NOT of THIS WORLD

AN INVITATION TO THE SECRET PLACE,
Intimacy with God, and His Lordship

ANDREY SHAPOVAL

NOT OF THIS WORLD: *Invitation to the Secret Place, Intimacy with God, and His Lordship*
Copyright © 2024 Andrey Shapoval

Translated and published by Andrey Shapoval Ministry International
Predestined department team: Lubov Kasyanov, Alona Makouchev, Andrey Kasyanov, Tanya Smirnova, Claudia Dulude
Cover design: Max Banmann, Lilit Hasratyan, Aleksey Kaznacheyev
www.shapovalministries.com
For more information on international distribution visit: www.ffministry.com/books

No part of this book may be reproduced without written permission from the publisher or copyright holder, nor may any part of this book be transmitted in any form or by any means electronic, mechanical, photocopying, recording, or other, without prior written permission from the publisher or copyright holder. All rights reserved.

This manuscript has undergone viable editorial work and proofreading, yet human limitations may have resulted in minor grammatical or syntax–related errors remaining in the finished book. The understanding of the reader is requested in these cases. While precaution has been taken in the preparation of this book, the publisher and author assume no responsibility for errors or omissions or for damages resulting from the use of the information contained herein.

Unless otherwise noted, all scripture quotations are taken from the *New King James Version*®.
Copyright © 1982 by Thomas Nelson. Used by permission. All rights reserved.
Scripture quotations marked NLT are taken from the *Holy Bible*, New Living Translation, copyright © 1996, 2004, 2015 by Tyndale House Foundation and used by permission of Tyndale House Publishers, Inc., Carol Stream, Illinois 60188. All rights reserved.
Scripture quotations marked NIV are taken from *THE HOLY BIBLE, NEW INTERNATIONAL VERSION*®, NIV® Copyright © 1973, 1978, 1984, 2011 by Biblica, Inc.®
Used by permission. All rights reserved worldwide.
Scripture quotation marked KJV are taken from *King James version @1979 by Tomas Nelson*. Scripture quotation marked AMP are taken from the Amplified® Bible, Copyright© 1954, 1958, 1962, 1964, 1965, 1987 by The Lockman Foundation

Take note that the name of satan and related names are not capitalized. We choose not to acknowledge him, even to the point of violating grammatical rules.
Throughout the book the author has emphasized certain words within the Bible text with boldface.

ISBN: 979-8-9893650-1-2 paperback
ISBN: 979-8-9893650-2-9 hardcover

Table of Contents

Foreword 3

Where Did You Come From? 7

The Younger Son's Return 13

The Power of His Love 31

Life Under His Lordship 51

Jesus' Secret Place 75

What Was That? 93

Teach Me, Holy Spirit! 111

We Celebrate The Lord! 133

"I've Found a Man After My Own Heart" 155

The Breath Of God 173

Not Of This World 195

Stay Connected 221

Other Books 223

Let Your Kingdom come on earth!
Let Your will be manifested,
Let Your sons arise and roar –
We will rise together!

Let Your Kingdom come on earth!
Let the heavens touch the nations,
Let Your power fall on us –
We will rise together!

Andrey Shapoval

Foreword

On the grand tapestry of our lives, a profound truth often eludes us in the hustle and bustle of our daily existence: Being close to God is a choice. It is not dictated by God's whims, our ministries, or even our divine calling. Rather, it is a matter of our own volition, our resolute decision to draw near to the Lord. This truth forms the heart and soul of the chapters in Andrey Shapoval's enlightening and spiritually enriching book.

As a pastor, I have been privileged to witness countless individuals embark on their unique journeys of faith. I've also come to notice that a Christian's walk with the Lord can become distant when that believer is caught in a state of complacency in their relationship with Christ. It is undeniable that our outward circumstances do not solely determine our closeness to God but are fundamentally a reflection of our inner choices. In his book, Andrey Shapoval unpacks this profound concept, urging us to take responsibility for our relationship with the Creator.

Jesus Christ, the ultimate model of intimacy with God, extends to us an invitation to draw near. Just as He walked in unparalleled closeness with the Father, we are now called to follow suit. To live lives surrendered entirely to God's lordship and to advance His kingdom in the power of His Spirit. To dwell in this world but not be entangled by its snares.

Andrey Shapoval extends a clarion call to ministers and believers alike, challenging us to seek a deeper, more intimate relationship with our Heavenly Father. Shapoval's raw and moving personal journey of his walk with God offers invaluable insights into the lessons the Holy Spirit has imparted to him throughout his relationship with the Father. It ignites a flame to crave that constant connection with God and be wary of the stagnation that can take form in our relationship with Him.

God has wrapped us in His unconditional love in His boundless mercy and grace. He has never left us. Even when we run from His presence, He is still pursuing our hearts. This book is a passionate plea to let nothing hinder us from venturing into an intimate relationship with the Author of love. I have been pierced by the truths found in this book as it echoes the theme of James 4:8, "Draw near to God, and He will draw near to you…"

As you turn the pages of this book, may your heart be stirred, your spirit awakened, and your faith rekindled. May you, dear reader, heed the call to intimacy with God, choosing to draw closer to Him each day. "Not of This World" is an inspiring guide, a beacon of light in a world that often distracts us from what truly matters. It is a divine invitation to dwell in the presence of the Almighty and to live a life transformed by His love, grace, and unending mercy.

May your journey through these pages draw you nearer to the One who longs to be intimately known by you. May it be a catalyst for your own pursuit of a life not of this world but firmly rooted in our Heavenly Father's boundless love and grace.

Samuel Rodriguez
President of the NHCLC/CONEL
Best-selling Author of Be Light and
Persevere with Power
Lead Pastor of New Season, Sacramento, CA
https://www.pastorsam.com

Introduction
Where Did You Come From?

"Where did you come from?" a church minister stood in front of me, intently gazing into my eyes. "Who are you? I've never heard of you, yet I'm astounded by what God has done through you today. I've never experienced anything like this before."

It happened at a conference in Europe where I was invited to minister. During the final service, God's presence filled the auditorium while I was teaching. I sensed the tangible presence of the Holy Spirit descending in the room as I led people in corporate prayer. Many were baptized with the Holy Spirit and filled with the fire of God. The anointing and fire of God were so heavy on me that I immediately went down to the altar area to pray and minister to people. Soon, I ran out of time and had to hurry up to the car when this gentleman stopped me. His eyes were brimming with tears. His excitement was palpable; he yearned for more of God. He demanded an answer: "Where did you come from?"

With a calm yet resolute voice, I replied, "From the secret place of the Most High." My words perplexed him, and he remained rooted to the spot.

I didn't intend to garner attention, and I wasn't well-known among other ministers at that time. God is my witness; I wasn't after fame, a platform, or a pulpit. I sought to be known in the spiritual realm and in God's Kingdom. That is why I have been spending time with God in the secret place for years, seeking intimacy with Him and getting to know Him more and more. And as it's written, all that is done in secret will eventually be brought into the light.

When I devoted myself to the Lord in 2002, I set this one goal: To get to know God Himself. Even though I grew up in a Christian home and heard Bible stories all my life, I didn't know God personally or have a relationship with Him. That is why the day I truly repented and gave my life to God, I told Him: "For the past 22 years, I've heard about You but never knew You. From now on, I will do everything and more to come to know You personally." God knew that I was not talking about having a life of ministry at all. I was thinking about an intimate relationship with Him. And at that moment, I devoted myself to God, to Him alone for all my life. I intentionally started to separate myself from the busyness of this life, deliberately spending time with God and getting to know Him more. To tell you the truth, it was not easy. For the past 20 years, I kept my promise to Him and have made every effort not to get distracted by other things, even important things. I tried my best not to go astray and kept my eyes fixed on Jesus, seeking to please Him. I'm still fighting the allure of distractions to safeguard my time with Him and ensure that it remains my highest priority. It is not enough to simply acknowledge God as my Savior; I yearn for Him to be the Lord of every area of my life.

Did I become a minister? Yes, but the ministry is a result of my secret place, not the reason I go there. It's what God is doing through me, and it's the work of His hand. Hear me out: I do not serve the ministry. I serve God and am entirely devoted to Him, not the ministry. He does His ministry through me. I have realized that it is impossible to fulfill the will of God on earth solely by my strength and capabilities. Yes, His will is being done through us, but by His hand and not by our abilities or charisma. Surrendering to the Lord transforms our lives, as we are imbued with a sense of wholeness, and we become the channel that allows God to flow through us and do His works.

I will not teach you the fundamentals of prayer, prophesy, or exorcism in this book. Furthermore, I won't be covering the methods of successful evangelism, hosting crusades, or leading masses to repentance. You can start doing all of these yourself if you grasp the heart of this book. All I want is to show you how to return to the Father's house and have a close relationship with Him, understand the value of sonship, and be a man after God's heart so you can fulfill His desires on this earth. I will also share my mistakes in this book to prevent you from making them. I will share my experience and what God has taught me throughout many years, restoring me as a son in His Kingdom.

I believe God is raising His sons and daughters in this hour, and all creation is waiting eagerly for the Lord to reveal who His children are (Romans 8:19). Note that in the last days, it won't be simply believers who will be revealed—it will be the sons of God—who will bring His glory to this earth. Only a son or a daughter can see what the Father is doing and fulfill His will. Only a son or a daughter has a share in the inheritance. Only a son or a daughter knows the Father intimately and submits to Him willingly. Let me add this: The pinnacle of freedom is not independence from God but your wholehearted and total reliance on Him. He is the source of your breath, delight, destiny, inheritance, and calling. Therefore, sonship is directly connected to the will of God on earth and carries a different way of thinking compared to a slave's or a servant's mindset. Sonship is associated with maturity, a trait intimately related to your responsibilities in the Father's house.

In the Old Testament, the book of Isaiah reads: *"The voice of one crying in the wilderness: "Prepare the way for the LORD…"* (Isaiah 40:3). In the New Testament, we hear this voice again immediately before Jesus stepped into His ministry, *"Prepare the way for the Lord!"* (Mark 1:3). This passage reveals that God is waiting for us to prepare the way for Him. It is no longer people who wait for God. It is now God who waits for His people. He is waiting for us to prepare the way for Him on this earth. Yes, people waited on God in the Old Testament, but God is waiting on us in the New Testament. The Holy Spirit has already descended and dwells here in us. It is not God who is busy; rather, we find ourselves overwhelmed with our earthly existence.

Once, the Holy Spirit said to me: "I long for your presence more than you long for Mine. I want to have a relationship with you more than you do." These words shook me to my core. Just follow my thought: God initiated the fellowship with men; He first loved us, found us, chose us, and forgave us! He did it first! And He is waiting for us to present ourselves to Him, His ways, and His lordship so He can deal with our mindset and raise us as His children. The Holy Spirit prompts us to "prepare the way for the Lord, make straight paths for Him, make every mountain and hill low, fill every valley, and make every crooked way straight, for the Glory of God to be revealed."

If we allow God's Word to shape our way of thinking and make our crooked ways straight, we will see the glory of God revealed in our lifetime. Trust me, God wants to manifest His glory more than we want His Kingdom to come and His will be done here on earth as it is in heaven. We just need to surrender and seek a closer relationship with Him.

The secret place of the Most High, His lordship, and an intimate relationship with God—these are the themes of my soul, my heartbeat, and my spirit—to earnestly pursue Him, to know Him, to obey His voice, to be a man after God's own heart, to be His son, and fulfill His desires on this earth. This is where we are diving into this book. Are you ready?

Then let's GO! Full speed ahead!

Chapter 1
The Younger Son's Return

Jesus said to him, "I am the way, the truth, and the life. No one comes to the Father except through Me."

John 14:6

In 2002, after my encounter[1] with Jesus, I realized there is so much we don't know about God. This truth made me bold enough to cry to Him daily because I no longer want to live a mediocre Christian life! As I prayed, fasted, and remained in the Word of God, reading chapter after chapter, the magnificence of God's reality captivated my heart, igniting an unquenchable desire to know Jesus above all else. I wanted to know God personally; I yearned to know His heart intimately. I cried to heaven: "God, don't look for another man to reveal Yourself to. You found a man. You can have me! Reveal Yourself to me!" I was so

---

1 You can read my full testimony and supernatural encounters with God in my previous books "Predestined" and "Big God."

eager that I set my alarm clock to get up in the middle of the night to spend time with Him. I did this consistently. Night after night, I was pressing in to know Him more. My prayers were simple: "All I want is to be with You. Please, reveal Yourself to me. Share Your heart with me. I want to know Your will." As days, weeks, and months unfolded, God began teaching me, and step by step, through His Word, He was taking me deeper into getting to know Him.

Have you ever wondered what is in the heart of God? What is His desire? What did He have in mind when He created this world? What was His purpose for us? I believe Paul the apostle had similar questions because of the way he writes to the church in Ephesus:

> *Blessed be the God and Father of our Lord Jesus Christ, who has blessed us with every spiritual blessing in the heavenly places in Christ, just as He **chose us** in Him before the foundation of the world, that we should be holy and without blame before Him in love, having **predestined us to adoption** as sons by Jesus Christ to Himself, according to the good pleasure of His will (Ephesians 1:3-5).*

As you read, the Scripture clearly states that the Almighty's earnest desire was to adopt us as His own. In essence, He had preordained our adoption from the very beginning. Yes, that was God's longing from the start! That is His will. That is what is in His heart. He desires to adopt us as sons and daughters to Himself. And lo, He has done that! God proved His boundless love by giving everything to adopt you expressly as His own, a feat made possible only through the perfect sacrifice of Jesus Christ.

Isn't it fascinating that God did not reveal Himself as God the Father from the beginning? He simply could not do it in the Old Testament. However, he revealed Himself using many other names: Almighty, I AM, the LORD, Adonai, Elohim, and Yahweh. However, the Old Testament does not talk about God being a Heavenly Father. He could only reveal that part of Himself when Jesus Christ came to earth.

I Want to Adopt You!

Envision this: From the foundation of the world, God already saw you in this day and age, in your current location and situation, and His heart longed to adopt you. This mystery of God's will is revealed to us through Jesus Christ. He poured out His heart by saying: "I am the Father. I want to adopt you so you would be Mine."

It's good news, but knowing about it is not enough. What good is knowledge if we don't live by the revelation? It won't make a difference. Therefore, it is crucial to not only grasp the mystery of His will but apply it to our lives and keep growing in this revelation. As the book of Galatians says:

> *But when the fullness of time had come, God sent forth his Son, born of woman, born under the law, to redeem those who were under the law, so that we might receive adoption as sons. And because you are sons, God has sent the Spirit of his Son into our hearts, crying, "Abba! Father!" So you are no longer a slave, but a son, and if a son, then an heir through God (Galatians 4:4-7).*

In this passage, again, the apostle Paul is writing about adoption. Why is this important? Why is he turning the church's attention to this truth again? It's because starting from the third chapter of Genesis and to the coming of Christ, all of humanity was under the dominion of the orphan spirit. Take any time in history, choose any kingdom, and look even through the law and the prophets; you will see that the orphan spirit manifested itself in various ways. These manifestations serve as evidence that heaven had not yet adopted humanity. Why? Because the Spirit of adoption hadn't yet instilled the concept of sonship into people's lives. Adam and Eve's fall created a massive gap between heaven and humankind.

It took the sacrifice of Jesus Christ to consolidate humanity, to join the Father and mankind back together, and for the Holy Spirit to make that adoption real in people's lives. Simply put, the possibility of bringing unity to all things in heaven and on earth was only attainable through Jesus Christ, and making that adoption a reality in people's lives was only doable through the Holy Spirit. It is finished. Hallelujah!

Bear in mind that Jesus constantly fixed His gaze on the Father when he walked on earth. Everywhere He went, He always taught about the Father and the Kingdom of His Father. Jesus adored the Father and did nothing of His own accord; He only did what He saw the Father doing. Jesus directed His attention to the Father because He knew His primary purpose was to become the door through which humanity would be led and reunited with the Father; this was the assignment of the Messiah, Jesus Christ. Therefore, you can only access all the Father has promised us through the Son. Do not even allow the thought that your achievements, personality, good deeds, or spirituality could be the catalysts behind it. It's solely by the grace of Jesus. We should never forget the Cross and the price God Himself paid for us to be where we are now and have all blessings and promises available to us. May we never lose the wonder of Jesus, His victory, and His sacrifice for us.

Only one path allows people to walk closely with God: Jesus Christ. He said: *"I am the way, the truth, and the life. No one comes to the Father except through Me"* (John 14:6). When He said, "I am the way," He meant that He would be guiding us in a direction leading to a particular destination. Please note that Jesus isn't directing us to a Healer, Adonai, or Elohim. He is leading us to the Father. And my dear friend, that is our ultimate goal—to end up at the Father's house.

The Way to the Father

In the parable of the prodigal son, Jesus masterfully described our adoption process in detail. Many people quote this parable during evangelism to call sinners to repentance. Additionally, it's been subject to many other interpretations. However, this parable also unveils and manifests the mystery of the divine adoption process.

I'm sure most of you are familiar with the parable in Luke 15. It portrays a father and his two sons. The younger son, driven by a desire for independence, boldly decided to claim his share of the estate. So, one day, he took all his father gave him and embarked on a journey to a faraway land, where he recklessly squandered his fortune with his friends. Soon, he found himself caught in a dilemma. Then, verse 17 boldly declares that the younger son *came to his senses,* illustrating true repentance, being born again, and a transformation of his mindset. Wouldn't it be amazing if people started coming to their senses? Many believers, especially those born and raised in Christian families, often live for the opinions of others and are under other people's influence, just like the younger son. I often ask: "When will you begin to think for yourself? When are you going to start seeking the Truth? When will you come to your senses?" I want to tell these people, "It's time to start thinking about your life, calling, and destiny. Don't live your life according to somebody else's script. Come to your senses."

> When **he came to his senses,** he said, 'How many of my father's hired servants have food to spare, and here I am starving to death! I will set out and go back to my father and

> *say to him: Father, I have sinned against heaven and against you. I am **no longer worthy** to be called your son; make me like one of your hired servants (Luke 15:17-19 NIV).*

Indeed, it's commendable that the prodigal son came to his senses, but at that given moment, he was looking deep inside himself, scrutinizing his actions and past. Because he believed he was unworthy, the prodigal son was the perfect soil for the orphan spirit. He said: "I will return to my father, but I am no longer worthy. I will live in my father's house, but I will identify myself with the servants. I am not worthy to be called my father's son."

"I am no longer worthy to be called my father's son"—that way of thinking always works to the devil's advantage. The feeling or belief of being unworthy has infiltrated Christianity today. The enemy knows that as long as we consider ourselves as servants rather than sons, we will block our own access to our inheritance and authority and won't be able to fulfill our calling. Let me remind you again of the connection between sonship and our destiny. My friend, we need to recognize who we are, what we are entitled to, and what belongs to us in our Father's house.

And so the son returns with this conclusion: "I am no longer worthy to be called your son. I am going to my Father's house to be a servant."

Doesn't that sound familiar?

"I'm no longer qualified to have the rights of a son. The more I think of what I did, the more unworthy I feel. Okay then, I'll humble myself. I won't pray for other people."

"Oh, why not?"

"I just feel like I'm not worthy."

"But who said it was about you? Who told you this has anything to do with your feelings? Where did you get that from? Is it mentioned in the New Testament? In the Old Testament—yes, but not in the New Testament. Who got in between you and the Father? Whose voice got in the way?"

And God says:

"Son, that is not My will. That is not My heart. Understand that quite the opposite is true. I want to make you worthy and help you realize that you are My son. I long for you to step into sonship and fulfill what I made you for."

"No, God, I can't. I don't feel that way. I feel unworthy. I go to Your house every Sunday to relieve my burdens. Then, I return to being a servant and work hard, just like servants do. That is how I will humble myself to be saved and get to the doorstep of Your house."

Are these sometimes your words, my friend? Many believers are content with only making it to the doorstep of our Father's house. They are satisfied to be on the outside, looking in, but I might upset you with the following statement: There is no more room there. A whole line of people are waiting for the opportunity to sit on the edge of the doorstep.

And he arose and came to his father. But when he was still a great way off, his father saw him and had compassion, and ran and fell on his neck and kissed him (Luke 15:20).

Wait, what? The father's view of his son was opposite to what the prodigal son believed about himself then! *If only my father received me back as a servant, I would work day and night.* And at that same time, the father is looking in the distance and thinking, "If only my son knew my heart, if only he knew my will. I long to make him my son again. I want my son back. I have enough servants. I want my son to be with me. I don't need more slaves. I need my son." The father has an entirely different mentality and attitude toward his son.

At that moment, the younger son had a slave mentality. The son was walking back home, feeling completely unworthy. That is how he saw himself, but little did he know that his father's heart overflowed with compassion. It is worth noting that it wasn't the son who ran to the father, but rather the father who eagerly ran to the son! The same thing happened in the spiritual realm when Jesus declared on the cross: "It is finished." Our Father God tore the veil between heaven and earth from top to bottom and ran to humanity, embracing us as His sons and daughters. It's what He wanted all along!

Neither Orphan nor Slave

Do you know what is heartbreaking for parents who adopt a child? It's when the child still feels abandoned, pushing away love and any good thing because they feel unworthy. That happens because the adopted son or daughter never let go of the past. The father wants the adopted child to act like his legitimate son or daughter. He wants them to feel free to open the fridge, grab a snack, and enjoy it. But the mindset of an orphan and a servant will always question it, "Am I even allowed to do that?"

A true son acts differently. When my child is hungry, he flings open the kitchen door, dashes to the fridge, and takes whatever he wants just because he is hungry. He takes what belongs to him in the house. He isn't asking whether he is allowed to have food. I usually remind him, "Hey, don't leave the fridge door open. Clean up after yourself." I am not talking about entitlement here; I'm talking about the confidence that comes from being a son. Because he is my son in my house, he thinks, acts, and responds a certain way.

And the son said to him, 'Father, I have sinned against heaven and in your sight, and am no longer worthy to be called your son (Luke 15:21).

Remarkably, the father remains unfazed by his son's emotional expression of feeling like an orphan. The father says: "Hmm... he sees himself naked. Very well then, put the best robe on him so he can feel worthy and accepted."

*But the father said to his servants: "Bring out the **best robe** and put it on him, and put a **ring** on his hand and **sandals** on his feet" (Luke 15:22).*

Since the third chapter of Genesis, humanity has been in a state of nakedness. God is tired of that self-perception and the negative image that comes with it. That's why the father said: "Bring the best robe, so he would no longer see himself as naked. But don't just bring the best robe; put it on him."

"And bring the fatted calf here and kill it, and let us eat and be merry; for this son was dead and is alive again; he was lost and is found." And they began to be merry (Luke 15:23-24).

Here is the blueprint of our complete restoration.

In Eden

Right from the start, the devil had his eyes set on tarnishing the self-image of mankind and disrupting our relationship with our Father. In the first chapters of Genesis, we learn about Adam, a man who symbolizes all of humanity, plus his special bond with God in the cool of the day. There were no mediators, prophets, pastors, or apostles in Eden; there was God's divine presence, His voice, and there was Adam. Their relationship was founded on a deep sense of fellowship and trust.

Please note this: God's relationship with his son was not designed or built by man. Many Christians use the phrase "building our relationship with God," but it is incorrect. Let's return to the original blueprint of how God intended the relationship with man and what sort of fellowship God Himself wants to have with us. Man didn't create Eden; God did. He initiated the relationship with Adam. I will talk more about it in the following chapters, but for now, let's look at what took place in Eden:

Firstly, there was an attack on the relationship between man and God. Lucifer managed to infiltrate the relationship between the Father and the son, beginning to twist how man perceived God (see Genesis 3). *Did God really say?* If you have been giving in to such thoughts, beware, for they can lead you down a dangerous path, distorting God's image in your mind. This false image, in turn, will lead you to doubt His words and your trust in Him. In this place of Scripture, we see how an external voice got into the relationship of God and man, presenting the Father in a wrong and distorted way. This external voice—satan—implied that God kept things hidden from Adam and Eve and that they were lacking something.

Secondly, there was an attack on sonship. "I have to do something to become like God." With that thought, the adversary pushed them further towards taking certain actions; that is how satan planted the seed of religion. It's the thought of constantly needing to do things to be like God and to please Him.

"Hold on, Adam, I created you according to My image and likeness. You are already like Me. I gave you authority, dominion, and an inheritance. Who told you the opposite?"

Thirdly, Adam begins to hide from the voice of God. Because he lost his righteousness, he is now afraid of God.

Fourthly, through seduction and deception, Adam lost dominion.

Afterward, God drove Adam and Eve out of the Garden of Eden and sent them to toil the ground from which the first man was created. They had to work hard for their food and sweat for the subsistence of their mortal lives. It was a tough break; Adam had lost everything: the abundance of provision, purpose, and satisfaction. Consequently, envy was born. Tragically, the first murder took place when Cain killed his brother, and this cycle of violence only escalated from there.

The Return

In the same way that Adam lost everything, Jesus, the last Adam, restored everything to humanity. When we look closer at this parable, we see the fullness and goodness in the Father's house, that Jesus fully restored:

1. The Father's Love

When the prodigal son returned, **the father ran to the son** with open arms, eager for his voice to be the first one his son heard. He knew that if anyone spoke to his son first, their words could distort his self-perception. The father wanted to protect his son from the hurtful words of others, which might confirm his doubts and fears about himself and his relationship with his father. Comments such as: "Look who finally came running back. Did you have fun? Did you get enough? You lost everything, didn't you? We knew this would happen! You deserve it!"

The father rushed to his son and showered him with his love, a love that covers many sins. Do you see that God the Father sees you differently? He has been longing to adopt you as His own from the foundation of the world.

2. Sonship

The second thing that the father restored is his sonship. Note that the prodigal son didn't have to earn it. He didn't have to impress his father by crawling to him in tears. He didn't have to work for it or do anything special other than come back to his father. The sonship is restored when the father embraces his son with open arms and welcomes him back.

3. The Best Robe

Now, picture this: The father lovingly clothes his son with a garment that symbolizes righteousness. He said to his servants: "Bring the best robe." There are different types of clothing, but the father asks for the best robe and puts it on his son because he prepared it for him from the foundation of the world. The best robe is a glimpse into the future, a foreshadowing of the Lamb, who was slain from the foundation of the world. He kept that robe for a long time, the best one He had, so He could put it on you.

If God Himself clothes you, who would give us the idea to take off what God places on you? What motivates you to unclothe yourself? Either you or the devil always tries to oppose God and take that robe off. Satan tries to unclothe man emotionally and spiritually.

God clothed us in the best robe. We are clothed in Jesus Christ. We no longer feel unworthy of Him because the Father sees us through Jesus. He sees us clothed in His righteousness. Now that you wear His robe, this garment shall never be stripped from you, even when you slip or fall. The first gift God gives us is not the gift of the Holy Spirit; the first is the gift of righteousness. My friend, righteousness is a gift from

God that will never be taken away. I can't emphasize this enough: God doesn't take away the gifts He gives us. These gifts have nothing to do with our emotions or feelings but are intrinsically linked to the essence of who we are clothed with. It's all about His magnificence.

Therefore, your identity doesn't change when you fall or sin. You are still wearing the robe of righteousness, and that righteousness will lift you higher. When you stumble, you rise with unwavering resolve because you still possess this precious gift your Father bestowed upon you. Just don't confuse it with intentionally living in sin. That's not what I'm talking about. If you sinned and sincerely repented, do not let your past stop you from ministering to people. You don't minister because you consider yourself worthy of ministry or better than those in need. It's not about you; it's about the One Who ministers through you.

Why is it that when we get sick, we learn to declare: "I am healed," but when we stumble into sin, we begin to say: "I am a sinner. I am not worthy." It could be our mindset and proclamation that keeps us down. By your words, you will be either justified or condemned. If you slip, remember what God has clothed you in. You are clothed with the gift of righteousness, and God sees you through His Son Jesus. That's why when you slip or fall, you should say: "This is not my place, nor my nature. I do not belong here. I am righteous." When you do this, that robe of righteousness begins to lift you up. You can't be worthy on your own; it is given to you. Jesus has earned it and given you the gift of worthiness, positioning you within Himself. Therefore, keep moving forward!

4. The Ring

When you are righteous, you get your dominion back. Prophetically speaking, it represents the Father saying, "Put a ring on his finger. He lost it when he left Eden." The ring represents dominion and authority. It's a sign of power, which Adam lost.

God can entrust you with His power when you are restored in sonship and righteousness. But what is that power and authority for? That is why, after placing a ring on his son's hand, the father says, "Put shoes on his feet."

5. The Shoes

Shoes symbolize purpose. The father puts sandals on his son, and in doing so, he restores him to his purpose. Those are the shoes to share the gospel. The son is given the authority to tread upon serpents, scorpions, and all the enemy's power, and nothing shall by any means harm him. The son has also been granted the authority to fulfill his calling. However, for the son to do that, he needs provision.

6. The Provision

The father says, "Bring the good fattened calf and kill it. Let's feast in the presence of the enemies, those who gossiped about him, and those who have been harassing my son. Set the table in front of all of them." That represents our provision.

7. Delight in God

"If the table is set, let's celebrate! Let's rejoice and dance with our whole hearts." Joy is a sign of delight and satisfaction in God Himself.

When Adam was banished from Eden into the world, he stepped into an unfamiliar world. Gone were the days of abundant provision; he had to carve his path in this new, challenging reality. But now the father is saying, "Son, let's celebrate. There is a good reason for it. Who cares if it irritates others? Let's rejoice and celebrate!"

Friend, the number 7 represents the fullness of God. Isn't it interesting that seven key things occurred in the Father's house?

The Sons of God shall be Revealed

Everything in life has its spiritual process: You cannot become a son if you do not encounter the Father. You won't be able to fulfill His will without His love. Starting from the third chapter of the book of Genesis, the relationship with the Father was regrettably severed through a course of events. However, when Jesus comes, He restores everything to how it was before, undoing everything sin did. He was the last Adam who restored God's love, sonship, righteousness, dominion, purpose, calling, provision, and satisfaction. Jesus showcased the heavenly model of restoration.

If only we could wrap our heads around the riches waiting for us in our Father's house. Although the prodigal son wanted to come back to the father's house, he didn't want any of what he was entitled to. Do you have any idea how many believers in the Father's house today still haven't accessed His goodness? Do you know how many orphans there are today in the Father's house? Why is this?

Isaiah 53:6 says: *"All we like sheep have gone astray; We have turned, every one, to his own way; And the Lord has laid on Him the iniquity of us all."* Where did we go astray? We have been wandering away aimlessly. Living in a fog in our way of thinking, we lost our purpose. We have been missing the mark all along. But there's good news: Jesus has already set us free from this way of thinking, so now we can finally step into our purpose and calling as sons and daughters of light.

Jesus said, "I am the door to the Father" (see John 10:9). But for some reason, many people still stand at the door. They settled in. We must recognize the significance of entering through Jesus and taking the next step, experiencing the profound embrace of the Father's love, sonship, righteousness, dominion, purpose, provision, delight, and satisfaction.

God, worldwide, has been restoring an understanding of sonship, which connects us with our inheritance and the fulfillment of God's will. Sonship will be restored. Sons will return, just as the prophet Isaiah wrote:

> *For behold, the darkness shall cover the earth, and deep darkness the people; but the LORD will arise over you, And His glory will be seen upon you. The Gentiles shall come to your light, and kings to the brightness of your rising. Lift up your eyes all around, and see: they all gather together, they come to you; your sons shall come from afar, and your daughters shall be nursed at your side (Isaiah 60:2-4).*

The sons are coming back to the Father's house. God is restoring true sonship in His house. The sons are being revived. They will no longer be after their own ambitions, ideas, ministry, and understanding, and they won't be driven by fear anymore. They will go and liberate all creation and liberate it from slavery into the glory of God's sons.

I want to prophesy to you today:

The younger son is returning, and that represents the next generation.

The next generation will be captivated by **the love of the Father!**

The next generation will be restored to **sonship**, and they will know their true identity!

The next generation will be clothed in **righteousness**!

The next generation will walk in **dominion** and tread upon serpents, scorpions, and all the power of the enemy, and nothing shall harm them!

The next generation will have God's **provision**!

The next generation will **delight** in God and **rejoice and praise** Him!!!

Father, I pray for every person reading this book right now. May they come to their senses. May every yoke in their life be broken by Your anointing. May the slave mentality be destroyed, may every bondage of satan be broken, and may this anointing begin to teach them from within. Captivate them with your love.

I pray that many mature ministers will arise—Your sons and daughters—those whom You will guide and who will carry out Your desires. They shall rebuild the old ruins, raise the former desolations, and repair the ruined cities, the desolations of many generations. They shall be called trees of righteousness, the planting of the Lord, that He may be glorified. May they please You, Father, with all of their lives, in Jesus' name.

I want to bless you and release the anointing and God's promises over you right now into every area of your life: spirit, soul, body, heart, mind, thoughts, feelings, emotions, will, finances, marriages, families, and homes. May the blessings you have received from heavenly places fill your life, expelling every sorrow, and may this anointing flow into your life. Receive it in Jesus' name.

Chapter 2
The Power of His Love

> *But God, who is rich in mercy, because of His great love with which He loved us...*
>
> *Ephesians 2:4-6*

I grew up without a father. My dad tragically died in a motorcycle accident when I was 5, so I never knew what the bond between a father and a son looked like. I didn't have anyone to show me what it was. I went through many different seasons of my life alone. I didn't have a father who would sit me down, talk with me, give me advice, or point me in the right direction. I observed my friends' relationships with their dads. Even though I enjoyed watching them, I knew deep down that I would never have that experience and that I had to be independent, without anyone to lean on.

I find it fascinating that during my supernatural encounter with Jesus —which you can read about in my book Predestined—the first thing I encountered in God was the Father's love for me. At the time, I didn't understand why Jesus held my hand, played with me, or sat me in His lap, but it was for a reason. As well as He knew my past, He saw my life years in advance, and He knew that for me to fulfill His will and minister to people, I would have to encounter the Father's love firsthand. That's why Jesus was ministering and loving on me, just as fathers do with their children. It was my first time encountering and experiencing the Father's love in such a mighty way. His love pierced my soul deeply and left an indelible mark in my heart.

The Breath of God

During my encounter with Jesus, He started to breathe into me. He began to breathe His own breath into my lungs, and when He exhaled, the fire of the Holy Spirit passed and flowed through my whole body— it was filled with His life and anointing. I was trembling. I still don't know how long it lasted because time feels completely different in that realm. But I clearly remember Him saying to me, "The time will come, and I will send you all over the face of the earth to minister to My Body with this anointing. My breath that's in you; you will breathe it into my people." As I received His breath and listened to His voice, His love filled my whole being.

God's love is the most extraordinary power ever to exist. Every time we encounter God, we come into close contact with His love because that is who God is. Don't get me wrong, I love the fire of God, His power, and anointing, but His love is greater than anything I've ever experienced. His love helps me live my life radically for Him and serve

His Body. No matter how charismatic or talented a person might be, God's love is the only effective way to minister to people. The love of God is the foundation upon which I build everything in my life. I firmly believe that everything we do should be built upon it.

When people experience His love firsthand, it marks their lives forever. God becomes so real to them that they can no longer keep it to themselves. Jesus stops being just a myth, and Christianity stops being a religion. Moreover, His presence becomes more real than all visible things! When we know God as our Father intimately, we will keep returning to Him because He is the ultimate source of life. He alone can understand, embrace, heal, and transform us. No earthly father can love and bless us like our Heavenly Father. More than that, He wants to do more for you than you can ask, think of, or imagine. His plans for you are good, pleasing, and perfect, and He has a unique design for each of us!

It hit me: God is my Father and I am His son. His love was imprinted on my heart and my mind forever. After that encounter with Jesus, I kept telling Him: "God, I want to return to Your presence. I just want to be with You." I never sought supernatural experiences; I just had this one goal—to come to know God Himself closely. I kept devoting my life to God every day, and little did I know that my desire to know Him would pull me out of a bottomless pit and bring blessings into every area of my life.

His Voice

The first couple of weeks following my encounter with Jesus, I could still smell the fragrance of heaven in my room while I was praying and spending time with God. I will never forget the scent of heaven; it became a part of me. I continued seeking God and asking Him:

"God, show me what I need to do."

"Seek My face," He replied.

"For how long?"

"Till your very last breath."

"But what does it mean to seek Your face?"

"My face is My voice. You will find it in My presence," He replied.

So, what does it mean to seek God's face? At the beginning of Genesis, we see God's voice was in the Garden of Eden. The book of Genesis says:

> *And they heard the sound of the LORD God walking in the garden in the cool of the day, and Adam and his wife hid themselves from the presence of the LORD God among the trees of the garden (Genesis 3:8).*

It turns out that His face is in His voice. His voice is in His presence. God is the Spirit. He wasn't walking in a physical body in Eden. Look it up. God didn't step on His two feet to meet with Adam; He would come with His voice. And after Adam heard God's voice, he said, "I heard Your voice, and I hid from Your face."

Back in Eden, Adam was complete: He was in perfect harmony with the Spirit of God. Therefore, it was natural for him to know and understand God's voice. Adam never confused God's voice with any other voice. For Adam, God's voice was clear and easy to understand. However, when God asked, *Adam, where are you?* Adam responded, *I hid from Your **face**.* So, to seek His face is to seek His voice, which is in His presence. In His voice, there is knowledge and wisdom, light and power. Knowing God's voice and getting to know Him closely should be the center of our prayer life. Instead, during our prayer time, many of us intercede for our needs, assuming this is how we seek God's face and pursue His voice.

> *Then the Lord God called to Adam and said to him, "Where are you?" So, he said, "I heard Your **voice** in the garden, and I was **afraid** because I was **naked**, and I **hid** myself"* (Genesis 3:10).

I want to draw your attention to the following: when Adam was deceived and believed the lie, all of a sudden, he became afraid of God. Similarly, many people today who have made bad choices, sinned, and screwed up are scared to return to the Father. If they were honest, many fear that God might speak to them. Like Adam and the younger son, many Christians believe they are naked, unworthy, and lost. This cycle keeps happening because believers don't get to know God Himself. Furthermore, they don't know their Father's heart and never come to know Him personally.

> *Who told you that you are naked?*
>
> *Have you eaten from the tree of which I commanded you not to eat from?*
>
> *Have you bought into the lie of the enemy?*
>
> *Who did you believe?*
>
> *Who told you this?*
>
> *Whose voice got between us?*
>
> *Who got their way into our relationship?*

You know the rest of the story.

But when the fullness of time came (Galatians 4:4), God sent His Son to restore the lost sonship. Jesus became the door to redeem humanity, restore what the first Adam failed, enlighten us, and allow us free access to the Kingdom of God. Unfortunately, many believers consider Jesus their final destination. They don't realize that He wanted to lead them further, back to the loving embrace of the Father, the King of kings and Lord of lords. Jesus said, *"No one comes to the Father except through Me"* (John 14:6). *Comes to the Father* implies a restoration of fatherhood and sonship. We have been granted access to the Kingdom of God, His promises, and most importantly, to the Father, His heart, and nature through Jesus Christ. The access to His Kingdom also provides the potential to be transformed into His likeness.

Head Knowledge vs. Revelation

There is a bit of dilemma and confusion in Christianity today. Knowing that you are a son of your Heavenly Father is one thing, but becoming one and living as such is different. Many believers say they are children of God, but there's a significant distinction between simply declaring it and living it as the core of one's existence. I can't emphasize this enough, saying, "I am a son or a daughter of God" does not necessarily make it true in your life.

Mere words don't scare the devil. In modern Christianity, people proclaim it, sing about it, prophesy it, and jump and shout, "I am a child of the King," and then go home not living like one. Knowing that God says you're a son doesn't equate to living in sonship. Proclamation is essential, but if sonship doesn't manifest in your life, then it is just empty words. The devil will do everything to keep you from getting to know your Father closely, to never reflect on His nature, never enter into sonship, and remain in that stagnant, lifeless state.

That said, becoming a fully functioning and mature son doesn't happen overnight. It is a divine process in which we allow God to become our Father and to adopt us. If you adopt a child from an orphanage and explain to him that now he is your son, it will take some time for the child to comprehend what sonship means and fully embrace this new reality. It's normal for the child not to immediately feel entirely at home, even after all the adoption formalities have been completed. It will take time and effort to cultivate that father-son relationship and to see a visible change in the mindset and behavior of the child. Incidentally, the adoption process doesn't depend on the Father alone. The Father has done His part, but how the child trusts and responds to Him will determine the ongoing growth of the relationship.

Knowing you are a son of God is a step in the right direction, but letting God the Father adopt you is truly an act of surrender.

Getting to Know the Father

I believe the further we move in time and the closer the Church gets to its glorious state, the more the Holy Spirit will lead us into the knowledge of the Father through Jesus Christ. Let me emphasize once more. It's impossible to get there without Jesus. I believe the Holy Spirit wants to immerse us into the Father under His lordship—but all this is granted through the Son. The further we move in time, the deeper we will come under the lordship of the Father through the perfect sacrifice of the Son.

You can only become a true son if you begin to reflect the nature of your Father.

Let's examine what Jesus Himself said about His Father. In Mark 10:17-18 it says that a young man came to Jesus, fell on his knees before Him, and said:

> *"Good Teacher, what shall I do that I may inherit eternal life?" So Jesus said to him, "Why do you call Me good? No one is good but One, that is God" (Mark 10:17-18).*

Interestingly, Jesus doesn't address his questions right away. Instead, he asks, "Why do you call Me good? No one is good except God alone"—that's what Jesus said about His Father. In other words, every good deed you have even known or seen being done by people around you or elsewhere cannot compare with the goodness of our Heavenly Father. No one is nearly as good as He is. Grasp this truth and let it permeate your entire being.

In another place of Scripture, He says:

> *If you then, being evil, know how to give good gifts to your children, how much more will your Father who is in heaven give good things to those who ask Him! (Matthew 7:11).*

Jesus paints a compelling picture here: "If you, being evil," in other words, "Guys, compared to the Heavenly Father, we all are evil, even when we do good, your nature cannot be compared to His nature…" Just imagine, all the good done on earth for the last six or seven thousand years can't even come close to the nature of the Father. If we combined every good deed and all the most remarkable human efforts to establish good, it would not come close to the goodness of the Father's heart and nature. That is why Jesus said, "No one is good—except God alone, the Father Himself in His nature."

I believe that God's nature will be revealed in a greater way in these last days. The revelation of His nature will give birth to the last Great Harvest.

His Great Love for Us

I am sure you have heard multiple times that God is good, loving, and holy, but I pray that through this book, God will take you on a profound journey of coming to know Him and experiencing His goodness for yourself. I pray that God will lead you as your Lord so you can start living your life from heaven to earth instead of vice versa. I pray that you understand your position of being seated in heavenly places and become the person God created you to be.

Please pause for a minute and ask God, *"Holy Spirit, reveal these truths to me. God, help me see this correctly and instill this revelation in me. Give me the Spirit of Wisdom and Understanding to come to know You more. Enlighten the eyes of my heart so I may know the glorious inheritance that You have for Your holy people. Help me to comprehend the immeasurable power of Your greatness in me and what I have been seated in heavenly places for. Amen."*

I want you to think about every word the apostle Paul wrote in Ephesians 2:4-6:

> *But God, who is **rich in mercy**, because of His **great love** with which He loved us, even when we were dead in trespasses, made us alive together with Christ (by grace you have been saved), and raised us together, and **made us sit together** in the heavenly places in Christ Jesus.*

Made us sit together, indicates Jesus's finished work and the position we are now in. It describes our rightful place in Jesus Christ. Do you know what position that is? It is far above all principality, authority, power, dominion, and every name. The Bible mentions it in Ephesians 1:20-23:

> *…He raised Him from the dead and seated Him at His right hand in the heavenly places, **far above all principality***

> ***and power and might and dominion***, *and every name that is invoked, not only in this age but also in that which is to come. And He put all things under His feet, and gave Him to be head over all things to the church, which is His body, the fullness of Him who fills all in all.*

Many believers admire the titles of apostles, prophets, and pastors, but those are just the gifts given to the body of Christ, not what we should strive to achieve or seek. The greatest position in Christ is not an apostle, prophet, pastor, or worship leader. The greatest position is being a son or daughter of God. Yes, apostles, prophets, and pastors have been given a measure of authority, but as sons, we exceed all rule, authority, power, and dominion.

Yes, there is a position in Jesus that is higher than all power, all dominion, and all other gods. You and I didn't earn this position. **Jesus earned it, seated us with Him, and gave it to you and me as a gift.** Jesus died with the old man. When He resurrected, we resurrected in Him as a new man, and He gifted us what He earned through His death. The grace given to us by Jesus is incomprehensible. We were raised to life in Him! There is no longer Jew or Greek, neither bond nor free, neither male nor female, for all are one in Christ Jesus, the fullness of Him that fills all in all. And that fullness is in His church in Jesus and under His dominion.

To understand that position, we need to look at the level of glory Jesus is in now. This will help us comprehend the glory we have been seated in:

> *And He put all things under His feet, and gave Him to be head over all things to the church, which is His body, the fullness of Him who fills all in all (Ephesians 1:22-23).*

Why would Jesus do all that? What for? Such an incredible price, such a sacrifice, such an unbelievable exploit. It was such a meticulous and demanding process and such a perfect ending. I remember there was a moment when the Holy Spirit said this to me, *It cost you nothing to have a relationship with Me. But it cost Me everything to have a relationship with you.*

God, who is rich in mercy, because of His great love — read it a hundred times if you have to and receive it.

Exceeding Riches of His Glory

He paid it all, ascended to heaven, and said, "I am not going to sit here alone. I will draw all people to Myself, and seat them with Me in heavenly places." Why? What for?

> *That in the ages to come He **might show** the exceeding riches of His grace in His kindness toward us in Christ Jesus (Ephesians 2:7).*

God wants to show, reveal, and manifest the exceeding riches of His glory and make them a reality in your life. There isn't a tape measure or ruler big enough to measure this grace. It's exceedingly abundant and immeasurable.

That is exciting, but grace is given for a purpose. There is grace for healing, deliverance, provision, and restoration. But it's interesting that when the apostle Paul talks about the nature of God the Father, he isn't mentioning healing, deliverance, signs, and wonders. He speaks about **showing the exceeding riches of His glory in the ages to come.** That is for us, our time period. Do you know how God's glory will be demonstrated? The Father will show His glory through His goodness, which will be poured out generously in the ages to come. It will carry healing, deliverance, restoration, and so much more! God will demonstrate the fullness of His nature, shaking our generation!

We see so much evil, perversion, immorality, depravity, epidemics, disease, conflict, and natural disasters in the world around us. All of that is the will of the prince of the power of the air, the spirit who now works in the sons of disobedience. He enslaves men, abusing their choice. The prince of the power of the air conquered creation by force. But do you think that only evil can express itself so vividly? No! Evil doesn't have the final say. The Bible tells us that the whole earth will be filled with the glory of God. The earth won't be filled with evil. It will be filled with the knowledge of the glory of God! Let this truth consume you—the entire earth will be filled with the glory and knowledge of God (see Isaiah 11:9; Habakkuk 2:14). It means that there is going to be a massive wave of God's glory connected to the Last Harvest, sons coming back, the restoration of sonship, with His love and His lordship. What a glorious time it will be!

Some things happening in our world today bring fear into peoples' lives, and that fear causes them to run to the church for answers. But the upcoming global revival and the revealing of the sons of God have nothing to do with fear and anxiety. It may seem like fear took everything under control, but with God, even His enemies work for His plans and purposes. That is what happened in Egypt. Pharaoh thought he had control over the situation, yet he failed to understand that he was only used to make God's name known throughout the earth. (We'll talk more about Pharaoh later.)

The will of our Heavenly Father is different, and it's good, pleasing, and perfect. God will never impose His goodness upon you; He will gently encompass you. His goodness will never bind you; it will set you free. It will be the exceeding and immeasurable goodness of God that will release the spirit of repentance throughout the entire earth.

Do you know why Peter submitted Himself to God? It wasn't out of fear. It wasn't God's wrath or power either that crushed him. Jesus never forced Peter to become an apostle and follow Him. He never forced Peter to leave his business behind. I have difficulty understanding why some people say, "God made me do this…". I believe people who say this never came to know God closely. He never forces anyone; it's not in His nature. I don't blame those who see God this way. I understand that this is what you were taught, but this teaching doesn't correlate with biblical truth.

His Goodness Doesn't Force You

Let's take a look at the Gospel of Luke 5:3-11. Peter and his friends were fishing all night but didn't catch anything. Jesus then says to Peter: "Put out into the deep and let down your nets for a catch." Isn't that what they had been doing all night long? But that didn't matter. What mattered was Jesus revealing His grace and demonstrating the Father's goodness to Peter. When they let the nets down, they caught so many fish that they filled not one but two boats with fish, to the point that they began to sink. Peter, a seasoned fisherman, knew that such a catch was miraculous, so he and the other fishermen were astonished and filled with reverence and the fear of God. We must understand that when Jesus called Peter, He used fish as a metaphor to announce that they would become fishers of men. Prophetically speaking, Jesus showed that there would be a release of such goodness and grace that "the nets" would overflow with "fish," and we would crowd the Kingdom of God with souls.

I want you to understand that God's goodness has nothing to do with your strength, efforts, or the season you're in. I want you to see it the way God does. You might've worked and strived all your life. Still, if you realize your position in Christ and know your Father's nature, you will enter a new season full of revelation and knowing God closer than you ever have. The more you immerse yourself into intimacy with Him, the more this season will become your reality.

Peter worked hard all night; logically, he had no chance of a catch at that hour. You might've also worked hard, tried to operate in your calling, and did all you could, but there has yet to be much fruit and very little catch. The catch doesn't have anything to do with your effort. It has to do with the goodness of God, which will be revealed through Jesus Himself: immeasurable grace.

Imagine this: Peter, a man of strong will, found himself in a moment that would forever change his life. It's fascinating that as soon as Peter witnessed the goodness of God, he fell on his knees. Jesus didn't say, "Peter, fall on your knees, and worship Me". Jesus didn't force him to bow down and repent, either. He didn't tell Peter how sinful he was. Jesus never said, "Do you even know who I AM?"—none of that. Jesus simply **demonstrated** the **goodness** of the Father to His son.

Do you know what happened next? God's glory came all over Peter and his friends. Peter then falls on his knees and says, "Depart from me, for I am a sinful man."

Someone might ask:

> *Why would you fall on your knees, Peter?*
> *Why would you repent?*
> *Who forced you?*

It wasn't fear of hell or death leading you to repentance. Fear doesn't save. Then what made you do so?

Truly, fear enslaves people. For those of you who try to bring people to repentance by fear and intimidation, forgive me for saying this, but you have not yet come to know God. You know some things about God but don't have intimacy with Him and have not come to see the heart of the Heavenly Father. Some people, however, will get saved by fear, but that isn't God's plan of revival. There might be cases of people coming to God out of fear of death and hell, but the global revival in this generation is coming back to God because of His goodness, not fear. The spirit of repentance doesn't carry the fear of hell and upcoming tribulations but the outpouring of God's goodness and grace.

Friend, only the Holy Spirit can open your eyes so you see your true self as God sees you. God finished it all. He already revealed His glory and goodness through Jesus Christ in the ages to come.

God's Goodness Embraces You

I prophesy that God will reveal His goodness in such a powerful way to this generation that it would not matter how much the devil would enslave them—God will set them free. God's will is the complete opposite of the enemy's plan. God's will is good, pleasing, and perfect, giving people hope and a future. God's will is all about His goodness—that's the heart of God.

The sheer number of attacks the enemy uses to enslave this generation is quite apparent. The internet has provided 24/7 access to various temptations that captured and enslaved peoples' mindsets. Today, young people are captivated by countless distractions, leading to an all-time high number of people enslaved to sin. The devil is banking on his strategy to redirect people's attention from God to sin.

Nevertheless, the apostle Paul says that when sin increases, grace abounds much more (see Romans 5:20). Sin increases through different tools and vessels. And while it seems like sin is prospering at full speed, the Bible says that the Holy Spirit will open endless doors, and His grace will increase **much more**. Again, all of this will be powerfully demonstrated through God's goodness.

I firmly believe God's goodness will captivate this generation's attention to the point that they will choose God despite all the evil opportunities and available temptations. It won't be fear, wars, natural disasters, epidemics, or earthquakes that will humble this generation, but God's goodness will make people willingly submit to Him. People will start seeking God, and the Father will reveal His nature and how dearly He loves them.

You're Saved, but What's Next?

Salvation is just the starting point. Many people receive salvation but never go further in God through the divine adoption process, coming to know God closely, growing spiritually, and being transformed into His image. Those steps must follow salvation. As it is written in Galatians:

> *Now I say that the heir, as long as he is a child, does not differ at all from a slave, though he is master of all (Galatians 4:1).*

That means we should let go of childish ways and start growing and maturing. Childhood represents immature Christianity that is focused solely on themselves and their salvation. Their goal is only to reach heaven's gates. However, the path to spiritual maturity is knowing God closely, growing in Him, understanding how He thinks, and knowing His will. **Maturity is connected to responsibilities in the Father's house.** By the way, that is why some Christians are not interested in growing spiritually; they realize that it will bring them into greater responsibility. We should never become content with only being saved; instead, we should grow from salvation into the lordship of God.

Let's recall the parable of the prodigal son, which we talked about in the first chapter.

> *Do you think the older son knew the father's heart?*
> *Was he transformed into his image and likeness?*
> *Was he under the father's lordship?*
> *Did he understand the father's will?*

The answers are obvious.

One can live all their life at the Father's house yet never change their way of thinking. One can live with the Father and never get to know Him. One can be a minister and be in the Father's business with an incorrect mindset. One can minister yet not reflect Him.

Imagine what would happen if it wasn't the father but the older son who first greeted his younger brother. What if that is why many people don't want to go to church today? What if that is why many are afraid a prophet might approach them and expose their mistakes in front of everyone? You may laugh, but this is a genuine fear for people in conservative churches. Some people even pray that God wouldn't speak to them through the prophets. It's dangerous when people operate in a prophetic gift with an unrenewed mind. When this happens, what was meant to build and encourage a person begins to destroy him.

The Older Son

In that parable, the older son returned from working in the field. In other words, he went on mission trips, preached a lot, labored a lot, and is now on his way home, where it's usually calm, just the way he likes it. But not this time. When the older brother found out how the father treated his younger sibling, he didn't even want to come inside the house:

> *The older brother became angry and refused to go in. So his father went out and pleaded with him (Luke 15:28).*

In other words, the older son rejected the celebration made for his brother. He refused to walk into the fullness of it. I can picture the older brother standing at the doorstep with an upset, grumpy face. The father went out and called him:

"Son, come on in."

"No."

"Son, come on in. Your brother is back safe and sound!"

"No way."

What a powerful illustration. The older son is used to quietness in the house, with no disturbance, just like at a museum. It's scary when Christians get used to that barren silence and don't feel comfortable when prodigals return. It disturbs them more than it excites them. Things get lively when younger sons return to their designation and calling.

Even though the older son had been with the father all his life, he didn't know the father's heart, feelings, or thoughts towards his younger brother. The older son was never transformed into his father's nature. And that incorrect mindset resisted the fullness the father was willing to grant to his sons.

Forget for a second about how much you serve God. *Do you know the Father closely?*

There are so many believers today who received salvation but never moved any further in God. Their mindset has not been renewed, and they continue living as orphans, rejected and in religion. I don't want just to be called a son. I want to embrace my identity and sonship as a child of God. I want to operate in sonship, fully comprehending and experiencing its meaning. He is my loving Father, and I am His beloved son. As soon as that becomes a living reality, the Lord's Prayer (Our Father) truly comes alive.

Many sons in the Father's house continue to live like orphans. Oh, how I despise the orphan spirit!

The presence of an orphan spirit perpetually seeks to assign blame to others. An orphan spirit always sees others as better than oneself, inducing feelings of unworthiness, deprivation, and disadvantage. An orphan spirit always wants to prove itself and seeks people's attention. It's after a platform more than its purpose and designation. It's more willing to take a microphone than ready to take responsibility. It seeks attention more than anointing.

The orphan spirit forces you to be jealous of others.

The orphan spirit makes you feel unworthy.

The orphan spirit brings rejection and the spirit of poverty into your mind and life.

The problem is that the orphan spirit doesn't leave quickly. It takes a journey of faith and spiritual growth with God the Father to defeat the orphan spirit. However, there's something you can do about this spirit today: You can choose to cut ties with the orphan spirit. I believe the anointing of the Holy Spirit will destroy its bondage and power over your life.

Declare this with faith:

> *I renounce every orphan spirit in my life.*
>
> *I renounce every spirit of poverty and rejection.*
>
> *I renounce the victim spirit.*
>
> *I renounce all feelings of unworthiness, envy, and strife.*
>
> *I cut them off of my life. Come out of my life, in Jesus' name.*
>
> *Today, I am going to my Father's house. I will celebrate and continue to get to know Him more and more.*

Chapter 3
Life Under His Lordship

He who dwells in the secret place of the Most High Shall abide under the shadow of the Almighty.

Psalm 91:1

While driving this morning, I was praying, "Lord, I am Yours. I am sold out to You. I belong to You. Captivate all of me. I am all Yours!" That prayer has become my go-to prayer, way of thinking, and aim in life—to be a man after God's heart and live a life submitted to His lordship.

Although that type of life is exciting, it can also be challenging. I remember a season when my traveling schedule for the ministry was jam-packed. I had trips scheduled back-to-back in different states and countries to minister at conferences and churches. When I flew to Germany, my wife Natasha sent me a picture of our son Elijah. Back then, he was only two years old. As he was sitting on a couch, playing with his little toy cars, our TV was on, and a video of me preaching aired on a Christian channel. When Elijah saw me, he started crying. Natasha captured that moment on camera and shared it with me. When I saw the picture, my heart sank. I wanted to grab him, hold him tight, and spend time with him. I felt incredibly overwhelmed during the trip because I knew I needed to leave for another conference the day after I got home.

Don't get me wrong, I love ministering to people and preaching the Word of God, but I felt a father's pain then. That image of my son crying played on repeat in my mind. In addition to that, I was physically exhausted from my busy traveling schedule. Upon my return home, for the first time, I said to my wife:

"Natasha, I don't want to go anywhere anymore. I feel exhausted."

That same night, I had a dream. I saw myself standing in a kitchen preparing a meal. I was making lots of food to feed many people I was supposed to be hosting. While cooking that meal, I saw the image of my son crying again. Then I heard a voice that spoke to me saying:

> *Are you telling Me that you are tired? And you don't want to go and minister anymore?*

"God, I don't even have time to spend with my son," I replied.

> *Don't worry about him. I will take care of your son and your family. And to you, I will give strength so you can go where I send you and do My work.*

I woke up suddenly, and while still meditating on that dream, I immediately started packing for the next trip. In my dream, I prepared a lot of food. That meant many people would gather, and I needed to feed them spiritually. Yet, I didn't feel more energy or strength, as God promised me in the dream. I just prayed, "Yes, Lord, I am all Yours."

I boarded the plane, still feeling drained, and didn't want to fly and minister. To numb my thoughts and feelings, I opened the Bible and started reading it, not paying much attention to what it was saying, just mindlessly reading. Suddenly, out of nowhere, someone spilled hot water over my head. Ouch! I thought a flight attendant was passing hot tea to someone and accidentally spilled it on me. I turned my head to see, but no one was there. I could still physically feel the "hot water" running over my head, to my neck, into my back and arms, and running out through my feet. I sat down and relaxed. The "hot water" ran down my body, washing out all my weariness.

Instantly, I felt incredibly light and released from my worries and that emotional weight. I felt a supernatural surge of strength and energy, immediately boosting my mood! God's abundant life entered me and filled me up. I kept reading the Bible for the whole flight. When I reached my destination, I effortlessly preached and ministered to people all day. Furthermore, I couldn't fall asleep that night, not because of insomnia but because I had tons of energy. I was not tired at all! I felt the same way the following two days; I couldn't sleep for two more nights! God supernaturally cared for my natural needs.

I quickly learned that when I present myself as a vessel to God, I experience His provision and care in every area of my life. He is the Lord of my life. He is the Lord of my family. He is the Lord of my children. When He sends me to do His will, He doesn't only take care of my financial needs. He takes care of all areas of my life so I can follow His call. That is why I'm no longer concerned about circumstances or obstacles, and I can boldly offer myself as a living sacrifice. It is written:

> *I beseech you therefore, brethren, by the mercies of God, that you present your bodies a living sacrifice, holy, acceptable to God, which is your reasonable service (Romans 12:1).*

When I surrender myself under His lordship, I can sense those moments when, during the sermon, it is no longer I who speak, but He speaks through me; it is no longer I who walk, but He walks through me; it is no longer me who minister, but He ministers through me. I'm still growing in my relationship with the Lord in the Holy of Holies, where the veil was torn into two, and access to the secret place of the Most High has been given to us all. I discovered that the structure of the biblical Temple in Jerusalem portrays a model of our relationship with God and our intimacy with Him. Let's take a closer look at its design.

The Temple's Structure

The Temple consisted of the outer court, the Holy place, and the Holy of Holies. Each section had different functions and things going on and was separated from one another by thick veils or curtains. This blueprint bears significant importance because it represents the different levels of intimacy with God we can have. The Temple's primary and most important purpose was to serve as a place where the glory of God dwelled on earth among His people.

The Outer Court was massive in size. It was the place where all the assembly would gather. This court, including Solomon's porch, served as a gathering place for teaching and instruction. It was open to anyone to enter, pray, or offer a sacrifice.

Unfortunately, many Christians have halted their journey at the outer court of their relationship with God and only accepted the forgiveness of sins from Christ's finished work. Many have received salvation and are content with that. But that is only the outer court of our relationship with God! Let me ask you this question, "Did you receive salvation?" If you did, great. But what's next? Did you receive healing and deliverance? If you did, great, but what's next? Did God bless and provide everything for you? If He did, great, but what for? Many believers just want to receive from God and don't see anything beyond that point. It often feels like many believers live their lives just to get saved, just for things to get a bit better, and just to have a blessed assurance. In other words, "Me, myself and I…it's all about me." Then, when some believers arise and go deeper in God, pressing forward, sharing the gospel, going on mission trips, and beginning to stir things up, the former would oppose them with a simple question, "But why? Everything is fine. We are saved, Jesus will come back and take us to heaven, we'll soon leave this world."

It has become common in many churches to continually preach sermons about maintaining our salvation. Why are we so focused on simply holding onto it? Could it be because someone taught us that all of a sudden, the rapture will happen? Could it be because someone warned us that we'd see a flash of lightning and hear that long-awaited trumpet sound, and all who are ready would ascend into the heavens while others would be left behind? Such teaching focuses people's attention exclusively on their salvation and the rapture.

Hold on a second. What if everything won't happen as it has been presented to us? What if the rapture is different from how we always imagined it? We somehow devised this concept *from salvation to rapture*. But what if that is not the case? What if the Lord waits for us to do something while we are waiting for Him? Did you know that God is attentively awaiting for us to come to know the truth and begin to do His will? The apostle Paul speaks about it:

> *God our Savior desires all men to be saved and to come to the knowledge of the truth (1 Timothy 2:4).*

Amazing, isn't it? His desire is not just for all men to be saved but for ALL TO COME TO THE KNOWLEDGE OF THE TRUTH. That is why the main focus of Christianity should never be just on maintaining salvation and church attendance. We must go further to His full knowledge and His will.

Have you ever noticed that Jesus never taught about salvation? He gave it as a gift. What was He teaching about? He taught people about the Kingdom of God and the renewal of their minds. Why? So that after a person receives salvation, they can understand the purpose of it and everything that comes after it.

Friend, I want to encourage you to pursue God and His will after receiving salvation. This is only the **outer court** of our relationship with God. Let's press on and move forward.

The Holy Place or Inner Court was a sacred place of service unto God. Worshiping, ceremonies, offerings, and sacrifices would take place there. Levites, the chosen tribe, ministered to God there every day. People would go there to offer sacrifices for forgiveness, thanksgiving, vows, and voluntary offerings and to receive blessings. The Holy Place was where the priests' services were made available to people.

In the Old Testament, the priest's duty was to offer sacrifices and work for God. The Holy Place was a hub of constant ministry movement and activity. Still, no matter how crowded it would get or the number of sacrifices offered, access to the Holy of Holies was strictly prohibited.

The Inner Court or Holy Place represents our relationship with God through what we do for Him. Many Christians get involved in church ministry and serving others, assuming they would get closer to God this way. They must realize this path is an outdated Old Testament form of intimacy. It takes them to the before the Cross era, where people tried to please God and get closer to Him using various works and efforts. I am in no way trying to diminish the ministry of the Old Testament. It was glorious (see 2 Corinthians 3:7-8). However, shouldn't the ministry of the New Testament, the ministry of the Spirit, the ministry on the other side of the Cross be more glorious now that the Lamb of God willingly shed His blood, the veil has been torn, and we have been given free access to the Holy of Holies?

I've heard numerous testimonies of people led by God to go on a mission or do some project for God. He blessed them, and they were successful. Then, for the next 20 years, they continue preaching and teaching others how to pray and serve God. Why? Because their attention is focused solely on ministry. They attract people to ministry so they can teach them how to serve God based on their perspective. I'm sure these ministers are notable, hardworking, and sincere, but how they present God comes from a place of doing things for Him. In other words, they are presenting God from the position of the Inner Court, the Holy Place.

Please understand: serving God is essential, but to be in ministry should never be the primary goal. Reflect on the teaching of Jesus: He did not teach about serving God; He taught about His lordship and His Kingdom. Ministry is just a means to God's end. We need to move forward in coming to the knowledge of God into the Holy of Holies, under the shadow of the Almighty.

Unfortunately, many ministers get comfortable in the Holy Place and focus on church programs and projects. Their lives are about serving God and people, and they never move further, just like an older son in the parable we read in Luke 15. I am sure that the older son was a **fantastic minister** and did many great projects, but he was never close with his father.

What if the devil wants to wear you out with serving, being busy for God, and being overly self-righteous? What if the enemy wished you never came to know your Father closely, His lordship, His will, so you would never go into the Holy of Holies?

When we get to the other side of the veil, to the Holy of Holies, it's no longer a matter of what we do *for* God but rather what we offer *to* God. And what He wants is us! He wants our bodies, our hearts, and our lives. Once that comes to pass, He begins to manifest and move through us, and we get to behold His glory.

The Holy of Holies

In the innermost section of the Sanctuary, you could find its most sacred enclosure—the Holy of Holies. The Holy of Holies was the dwelling place of God, and it was separated from the rest of the Temple by an enormous, heavy veil. Only the high priest was allowed to enter, and even he could only enter once a year! No one else, under any circumstances, ever had permission or access to it. The high priest would enter the Holy of Holies not with sacrifices but with the blood of a spotless lamb, presenting himself before the LORD.

It's fascinating that even today, Jews relentlessly ask God—in their Amidah prayer—for the restoration of the Temple and the service therein so that with its help, they **could achieve closeness with God** and have the opportunity **to fulfill God's will**. I want to clarify something here: The New Testament tells us that God tore the veil into two from the top to the bottom. It was beyond any human strength or capability to tear that veil. It was an entirely supernatural occurrence worked by the hand of God. The Cross of Jesus Christ was the shifting moment that changed the course of history and transformed the world forever, leading to the

New Testament. Free access to the Father, His presence, and the Holy of Holies has once again been given to humanity through the sacrifice and the torn body of Jesus Christ. We can boldly enter the Holy of Holies (see Hebrews 10:19-20) and live under His lordship to achieve closeness with God and do His will.

In truth, attending church services, helping in ministry, and even experiencing God's presence every once in a while is not enough for us to know Him personally. To get to know God closely, we must go further into the Holy of Holies. I want to note that God told Moses that He would **reveal** Himself and **speak** to him not in the outer court or in the inner court behind the second veil, where priests and Levites were serving. God wanted to do this behind the third veil—in the Holy of Holies over the Arc of the Covenant, from the mercy seat: *"[there] I will meet with you, and I will speak with you"* (see Exodus 25:8-22).

We don't enter the Holy of Holies with sacrifices and donations. We present ourselves as the living sacrifice in complete surrender in the Holy of Holies. That's where God will reveal Himself to you and lead you under His lordship, where you will hear His voice and follow it. In the Holy of Holies—you are the sacrifice. And if you don't reach that condition, He cannot become the Lord of your life. He can still be your Almighty God, but not your LORD. That's it. That's what it means to be under His lordship.

Allow me to clarify, "God" and "LORD" are not synonyms; they don't mean the same thing. God—is the higher power. LORD—is the one you submit to as your Master and your King, and you willingly choose His reign and will over your life above all else.

Pause and reflect on your life to see where you stand with God right now. What kind of relationship do you have with Him? Do you live under His lordship, or is He only your God?

Some would probably say, "Andrey, what you are saying right now is very serious. After all, many people are saved, involved in a ministry of some sort, pray to God, see healing, and walk in authority. Are you saying they might not live under the lordship of God and are still on the Old Testament side of the Cross?"

Exactly! That's why I can't remain silent about it. I want everyone to hear this. My dear brothers and sisters, this is not just my assumption. These are the words of Jesus Christ Himself, *"Not everyone who says to me Lord, Lord, will enter the Kingdom of Heaven…"*

Lord! Lord!

Let's look at this place of Scripture from the Sermon on the Mount:

> *Not everyone who says to Me, 'Lord, Lord,' shall enter the kingdom of heaven, but he who does the will of My Father in heaven.*
>
> *Many will say to Me in that day, 'Lord, Lord, have we not **prophesied** in Your name; Have we not **cast out demons** in Your name; Have we not **done many wonders** in Your name? And then I will declare to them, **'I never knew you.'***
>
> *Depart from Me, you who practice lawlessness! (Matthew 7:21-23).*

Pay close attention to these verses: Jesus isn't talking about eternal life in this context but rather emphasizing His divine lordship and authority. Also, He doesn't mention the category of people who referred to Him as Jesus, Savior, Teacher, or Healer, but those who call Him: "Lord, Lord."

What does this mean?

First of all, you can learn a lot of information about God, even know Him as your Savior (receiving salvation), as a Healer (when you get healed and even pray for others who will receive healing), as a Deliverer (when you get delivered), and yet still not come under His lordship and know Him as Lord. God becomes the Lord of your life when it's no longer you who has God to fulfill your needs, but God has all of you. The apostle Paul came into that position, which is why he writes: *"It is no longer I who live, but Christ who lives in me "*(Galatians 2:20). This is a process, and the more we come to know God, the further we go in this process.

Getting to know God is not about reading the Bible more frequently. Knowledge and revelation are not the same. Knowledge fills your mind, but coming to know God through revelation changes your life. God cannot be studied; He must be known. This is only attainable through unity with the Holy Spirit—also known as intimacy with God.

When you come to know God as a Healer, you encounter His Healing nature, and healing happens. So your knowledge about His Healing nature becomes more than just information; it becomes an experience that changes your way of thinking, and you begin to see sickness differently. Faith to heal begins to operate within you because you come to know God as a Healer. When you come to know God as the God who blesses you, you enter into His blessings, and they are manifested in your life. But to come to know God as your Lord, you must offer all of you; I'm talking about a living sacrifice, the Holy of Holies, and a different way of life. You won't be able to come to know Him as Lord if you don't offer all of yourself, every part of your existence. Only then will God be able to transform you and take you from one level of glory to the next, and your life will truly begin to reflect the image of Christ.

Secondly, not everyone who calls Him Lord lives under His lordship, but those who do His will. Please note that the words "do His will" are used in the present continuous tense, which doesn't mean that you do His will once or when it's convenient, but constantly doing His will. When we maintain a close relationship with God and position ourselves to know and do His will, it becomes our lifestyle and everyday way of life.

To fulfill the will of the Father, our focus should not be on ministry or people but on the Father alone. Why? You can do many things for God that He never asked you to do. So many Christians do a lot of good deeds, claiming to do them for God. That is not bad, but the question remains, "Did you hear from God? Did He tell you to do that?"

I'm convinced that there's a whole list of ministries that the Holy Spirit did not establish. People wanted to start a ministry, so they did. I'm also convinced there's a whole list of ministers preaching from behind the pulpit who God didn't appoint; other people did. I don't want to put much emphasis on this. My point is this: we need to do His will, not our own ideas that we think will help God. When you submit to His lordship, He tells you what to do, and you do it.

Thirdly, just because prophets heal the sick and cast out demons doesn't mean that they live under the complete lordship of God and are in the center of His will. It might hurt, but it's true! It is possible that someone can do all these incredible works but do them according to their own will, misusing their God-given power and authority. Let's go further. It might shock you, but prophecy coming true also doesn't indicate God's lordship in a prophet's life. Spiritual gifts continue to operate even when a person has not submitted to God's lordship. Why? Because God doesn't take back gifts. Sadly, I see it way too often. People use the name of the Lord and see good results, but they don't live under His lordship. In other words, He is not their Lord.

In Matthew 7:21-23, it talks about people who did things for God. They established ministries and performed signs and wonders but did not accomplish His will. They used God's name to build their name, reach their goals, and fulfill their agenda. That was lawlessness in God's eyes, "Depart from Me, you who practice lawlessness!"

Understand that the will of God is not only associated with the ability to prophesy, perform miracles, or do deliverance—all these things are needed and used by God to accomplish His will. They are necessary for the church, but they are not the goal. The will of God for the church is to fulfill its calling on earth, and that calling is directly connected with the lordship of God and the work of the Father.

Also, it is crucial to understand that God will not force His lordship on you. It is all up to you, my friend! It is your own choice to submit to His lordship. Whether or not you go further in God into the Holy of Holies is your choice.

Before we go any further, we need to understand something. The LORD is God's name, which He first revealed to Moses when He wanted to fulfill His will and manifest His lordship on earth.

Abraham and Moses

In Exodus 6, God appeared to Moses, saying:

> "I am the LORD. I appeared to Abraham, to Isaac, and to Jacob, as God Almighty, but by My name LORD I was not known to them" (Exodus 6:2-3).

The first time God reveals His name to a man is in the book of Exodus. Prior to Moses, He had shown Himself as God Almighty, the Creator, but never revealed His name. Not even to Abraham, who was a prophet, the father of faith, and a friend of God. Does it mean that Moses was more spiritual than Abraham? Did he deserve it more? Of course not! Then why? It has nothing to do with either Abraham or Moses. It's connected with the will of God and His timing. That's why we should spend less time thoroughly investigating the lives of Abraham or Moses to find the answers. Instead, let's dig deeper into the ways of God and see what His desire and goal was that He wanted to accomplish in that time period.

From Abraham to Moses, God was forming faith, so He revealed Himself as God Almighty. Faith, as we all know, is not established on words alone. It's also about witnessing the demonstration of God's power, miracles, and supernatural manifestation of His authority and dominion (see 1 Corinthians 2:5). Abraham is the father of faith. His way of thinking and faith was so remarkable that he called into existence things that hadn't even come to be yet. God chose Abraham to form faith in him, which he would pass on to his heirs, Isaac and Jacob, and through generations and generations. That was God's vision for that time. Works of miracles and the power of God were necessary to stir up faith in them. Moses also performed miracles, but God's will and focus weren't on forming faith in Moses' time.

Having faith in God Almighty will lead you to see miracles.

Having faith in God as LORD will lead you to do His will.

Pharaoh, You Thought You Were the LORD?

Now, let's look at Moses' pivotal time. Shortly after the Israelites moved to Ancient Egypt, Egypt became a global force that enslaved God's people. Before this happened, neither Abraham, Isaac, nor Jacob opposed the Egyptian dominion and its system. Therefore, God did not reveal Himself to them as LORD, which wasn't necessary then.

However, Moses found himself in a moment when God wanted to fulfill the promises given to Abraham and the people of God. Let's take a look at the book of Romans, where the Scriptures reveal God's way of thinking when He was fulfilling His will:

> *The Scripture says to the Pharaoh, "For this very purpose I have raised you up, that I may show My power in you,* **and that My name may be declared in all the earth"** *(Romans 9:17).*

This was God's plan. In other words, God was dealing with Pharaoh and the entire world system. *Why?* So that His name might be proclaimed in all the earth. *What name?* The LORD, the King of kings, God above all gods, the One who reigns forever! In other words, God was saying, "Pharaoh, I have given you your position to demonstrate My power. Do you think you are the Lord and rule over the whole world? No. I am the LORD. I will manifest My power over you. Through this, My name will be known and proclaimed across all the earth." I'm sure you know how the rest of the story unfolded.

We must remember that the Old Testament is a shadow of things to come. In today's world, Pharaoh represents the devil, and Egypt is the kingdom of darkness, the system of this world that enslaved people. God wants to get His people out of this system, sanctify them, and bring them into the promised land.

Compare this place in Scripture with Matthew 24:14. It says that in the last days, God, in a similar manner, will demonstrate His power and might for His name to be proclaimed in all the earth:

> *And this gospel of the kingdom will be preached in all the world as a witness to all the nations, and then the end will come (Matthew 24:14).*

And every knee shall bow, of those in heaven, and those on earth, and those under the earth, and every tongue shall confess that Jesus Christ is **Lord**, to the glory of God the Father (see Philippians 2:10-11). That sounds pretty exciting!

God Came Through Moses

No human power or ability could accomplish God's will on earth. God needed to do it Himself, with His hand and strength. To execute His plan, God needed a man to whom He could reveal Himself as LORD. Then, through that man, He would do His will. God handpicked Moses, setting him apart from the rest. Let me repeat: God chose Moses not for the service but for Himself, His lordship, and His will. These things are different. God did not need Moses's talents, abilities, skills, or education; He required Moses himself because He needed a person. By the way, Moses already tried to do God's calling with his own abilities and power back when he was 40 and still lived in Pharaoh's palace. Moses attempted to defend God's people and fight back against the system, trying to help God. As a result, he had to flee Egypt and forsake his calling.

However, at that moment, God stepped in to deliver His people. How? Through Moses. But this time, Moses submitted himself to God willingly. This is how lordship is manifested: I present myself to God as a vessel, a living sacrifice for Him to carry out His will through me. Let me reiterate: God did not want the ministry of Moses or the works of men; God wanted Moses himself, to do His will through him. It's as if God was saying, *I want you to be in sync with Me. When you go, I want you to obey all My words so you won't build your ministry but will be sensitive to My voice, My leading, and My will. For that to happen, I need you to dedicate yourself and be available for Me.*

The bottom line is that if Moses had not surrendered himself as a living sacrifice unto God, God would not have been able to demonstrate His lordship over Pharaoh through Moses.

Miracles Aren't the Point

God raised Moses in the eyes of all the people of Egypt, the Pharaoh, and the Israelites. Read the book of Exodus. No matter what authority or power Pharaoh used, the Lord was superior. When Pharaoh's magicians conjured up some snakes, Moses exercised great power over them, and his serpent devoured the others. That demonstrated to everyone God's dominion over all power. Remember that during Moses's lifetime, miracles were not the focus; the focus was on the manifestation of power to show supreme dominion.

The presence of signs and wonders in a ministry is excellent, but this is only a part of God's will. It doesn't mean His will is being fulfilled. Remember that miracles are only a manifestation of power. The Bible warns us that a person can do miracles in the name of the Lord and not fulfill His will. Someone can heal in His name and not fulfill His will. Someone can prophesy and yet have an unrenewed mindset. People can spend their whole lives prophesying in His name, casting out demons, and performing miracles, then hear, "Get away from Me. You were building your own kingdom, and you didn't seek to know Me or fulfill My will."

No matter how successful you are as a minister or how many miracles and healings happened through you, your greatness in the eyes of God is not in miracles and healings; what matters is the level of your dedication to Him and complete surrender under His lordship.

Those Who Saw Moses, Saw God

So the Lord said to Moses: "See, I have made you as God to Pharaoh, and Aaron your brother shall be your prophet" (Exodus 7:1).

These are the words of God, which means that Moses lived in such closeness with the Lord that soon both Pharaoh and the people began to fear him. *Why?* They saw God in him. Moses began to display the name of the LORD. This speaks of the oneness and unity Moses had with God. There was synchronization, trust, and deep connection between them. When we reach this level of intimacy with the Lord, we reflect Him and become an epistle that everyone can read. Jesus also said: *"He who has seen Me has seen the Father"* (John 14:9), *"My Father and I are One"* (John 10:30). This is only possible through knowledge of God and close relationship with Him.

Note that the people of Israel saw miracles and were impressed, but Moses saw the authority of God and His will. Also, it is essential to remember that God revealed His ways to Moses so that Moses would pay attention to the lordship of God and not just miracles (see Psalm 103:7).

Israel saw God's works, but Moses saw God's ways. Works are associated with the service of God, and the ways of God are related to the will of God and the knowledge of the LORD. If you give yourself to God, you will see His greatness and glory.

Are You Digging?

But why do you call Me 'Lord, Lord,' and not do the things which I say? Whoever comes to Me, and hears My sayings

> *and does them, I will show you whom he is like: He is like a man building a house, who **dug deep** and laid the foundation on the rock. And when the flood arose, the stream beat vehemently against that house, and could not shake it, for it was founded on the rock (Luke 6:46-48).*

I have a question: how much do you want to know Him as Lord? How much do you want to know His will? Are you digging? Are you going deeper? Or are you content with superficial Christianity? Digging and going deeper is what we are doing in this book, so please don't stop. Grab your shovel, and let's keep moving forward.

Sometimes people ask me: *"Why is that necessary?"*

Let me give you an answer:

How far you will go in God is determined by how deep you "dig" when you have time and the opportunity. How deeply you are rooted in Him is determined by how deeply you pursue relationship with Him, knowing Him personally and being transformed into His image. And do you know what all of that is for?

> *When the flood arose, the stream beat vehemently against that house and could not shake it, for it was founded on the rock (Luke 6:48).*

Floodwaters **could not even shake it**—not because you have built yourself a reliable business, a home, or a ministry. It's not because you have memorized all of God's promises and can recite them. You foundation is unshakable because you went deep into knowing God and rooted yourself in Him. And then, when the world experiences storm and shaking, when the land of Egypt gets overwhelmed with toads, lice, ulcers, and other plagues, every false foundation will shatter into pieces, but not yours. Everything and everyone will be shaken—everything and everyone but you. *The floods came and beat on that house but could not destroy it.* The kingdom of darkness and all its ranks came against you. They brought fear, depression, doubt, and deceit, unloading them on your property. Yet, through all of this, nothing affected you. Wow! What kind of lifestyle is it when visible things have no power over you and cannot shake you? It is a way of life when you and your house are under the lordship of the Most High, under His governance, dominion, and protection.

We can boldly sing together:

What a mighty God we serve,
What a mighty God we serve,
Angels bow before Him,
Heaven and earth adore Him,
What a mighty God we serve!

Your foundation is firm because you dug deep and built your house upon the rock. This lifestyle under His lordship is shown in Psalm 91, where we see the power of covenant, in which we grow under His lordship. (We will talk more about Psalm 91 later.)

Manifestation of Two Lordships

When the Lord brought His people out of Egypt, He demonstrated that a manifestation of two different lordships could occur at the same time, in the same place, and on the same physical territory. While some underwent plagues and horror, others rested in God's peace. That gives us a perfect picture of God's lordship demonstrated.

God's lordship was manifested over His people who were set apart for Him while plagues were happening all over Egypt. One group lived in a nightmare, while the other lived under God's supernatural protection. That protection was vividly and undeniably demonstrated for all to see. God set apart the land of Goshen under His lordship (see Exodus 8:22). And no one could refute the evidence of the difference between those who were and who were not under God's lordship.

The Bible says there was a great cry in the land of Egypt and peace in the land of Goshen so that not even a dog barked (Exodus 11:6-7). God's peace in His secret place under the shadow of the Almighty was evident to such an extent that even the dogs stayed quiet. Psalm 91 says, *"Only with your eyes shall you look, and see the reward of the wicked. Because you have made the Lord your refuge…"*. In other words, Israelites were looking out their windows and could witness the horrors happening in Egypt. The land of Goshen prophetically shows us what it means to live under His lordship.

End-Time Prophecies

Many end-time prophecies are going around in Christian circles today. I don't believe most of them; I don't even think they're from God. When believers use these prophecies to scare each other, move somewhere, or stock up on supplies, it shows they only see one side of the story. Their attention is not on the Lord and His plan, but on what's coming to Egypt. They spread fear for this reason. They don't consider what the Father is doing amid all of this. Remember, God will consistently demonstrate the difference, just as He did in Egypt—it was a night and day difference. While some were in darkness, others were in God's light. While some were defeated, others were redeemed and in peace. While some were under the lordship of Pharaoh, others were under the lordship of God Almighty.

Just as it happened in Egypt, so it will be in the end times: *"For behold, the darkness shall cover the earth, and deep darkness the people; But the Lord will arise over you, And His glory will be seen upon you"* (Isaiah 60:2). If you live under His lordship, you have nothing to be afraid of—you are in the light and under the shadow of the Almighty. God's glory will shine over His people, and darkness and horrors will cover the rest. God will protect and reign over His people while others will be defeated. Just as it was in the land of Goshen and the land of Egypt, it will be in the last days.

Let me finish my previous thoughts about end-time prophecies. It's not the different state or country you need to move to; it's the different lordship you must come under. Even in my home state of California, there will be those who live in "Egypt" while others live in "Goshen." I'm humbly saying this, having faith in the God I trust.

Please hear me: the future we are heading into will be a **terrible time** for some and a **glorious** time for others. God will again bring His people out of Egypt, and the things happening back then will also happen in the last days. What happened in the land of Goshen will be a reality for those who submitted themselves under the lordship of God. He'll do it for His name's sake, not because of you, but because you have known His name: the LORD. He will begin to manifest His name and His lordship.

YHWH

In this chapter, we've learned that Jesus' sacrifice gave us full access to the Holy of Holies, the very presence of God. It's where you present yourself as a living sacrifice to be under His lordship. It's where God sets you apart and reveals Himself to you. You don't come there once a year; you begin to live there—in the secret place of the Most High, under the shadow of the Almighty. This is more than just doing ministry; this should be your way of life. That's where you come to know Him as a Father and become one with His nature. In the following chapters, we will discuss the practical growth steps in this process. But I want to emphasize that this way of life isn't just about serving God. It's about coming to know Him closely, hearing His voice, and following where He leads you—becoming one with Him. In this, the lordship of God will be manifested.

Remember that God wants the entirety of your being; He wishes to be the Lord of all of your life. If you don't surrender completely, the offer won't be extended to you. In such a case, God will remain God Almighty for you, but not your LORD. That is a fundamental principle of His lordship.

And finally, the day the high priest entered the Holy of Holies was deemed the most important day of the year. This was the day of sanctification and union for the people of Israel with their Creator. The most important part of the day was when the high priest would enter the Holy of Holies to burn incense and sprinkle the blood of the unblemished lamb towards the Ark of the Covenant, saying the unpronounceable four-letter name of God: YHWH, which means the LORD. This is incredibly profound! He didn't say Almighty God, Savior, or Healer. He had to display the utmost sacred name—the LORD.

He is the LORD, and He will sanctify you for Himself in the Holy of Holies. There, you become one with Him, come to know Him personally through the adoption process, and embrace the privilege of becoming a son—by coming to know the LORD YHWH!

Chapter 4
Jesus' Secret Place

Learn from Me, for I am gentle and humble in heart.

Matthew 11:29

Here's a fascinating story about Jesus when He was just a young teenager. One day, Jesus' parents were visiting Jerusalem, and somehow, they lost track of Him. He was still young, just 12 years old. With great sorrow, they searched for Him for three days until they finally found Him in the Temple. You might have already heard this story from Luke 2, but it is worth mentioning again because it is the sole instance in the Bible where Jesus' youth is recorded. Remarkably, at 12, Jesus already knew Who He was, what He needed to do, where He needed to be, and what He was called to accomplish. However, just because He knew He was the Son of God did not mean that He matured in Sonship. Just like it's written in the book of Galatians:

> *Now I say that the heir, as long as he is a child, does not differ at all from a slave, though he is master of all, but is under guardians and stewards until the time appointed by the father (Galatians 4:1-2).*

Just like with Jesus, there's a particular time appointed by the Father for you, too. From an early age, Jesus knew He was God's Heir and Son, but He needed to mature into that position. Without that process, a person cannot fulfill the perfect will of God and the work of the Father. Someone might say, "Wait, how could Jesus be in an immature state? He is the Word that became flesh. He is God. The Teachers of the Law were astonished at His understanding and wisdom." Luke 2:47 says, *"Everyone who heard him was amazed at his understanding and his answers."* While all of that is true, Jesus was also the Son of Man who had a physical body just like us and had to resist the flesh and its desires just like we do. See, He had to grow and mature to become Who God the Father wanted Him to be. Jesus had to go through all the different seasons of life as we do. He needed to grow and mature, and maturity isn't determined by knowledge and revelation only. In fact, a person can be immature and still know a lot about God, start a ministry, or even teach others.

Let's look at Jesus' life from his early teenage years to when He embarked on His ministry. The concluding verses of the second chapter of Luke provide insight into the events that happened over the next 18 years:

> *Then He returned to Nazareth with them and **was obedient to them**. And his mother stored all these things in her heart. Jesus **grew** in wisdom and in stature and in favor with **God and all the people** (Luke 2:51-52 NLT).*

In essence, Jesus willingly submitted Himself and was obedient to the guidance of His earthly parents until the appointed time designed by the Father. This all correlates with Galatians 4:2—*"but is under guardians and stewards until the time appointed by the father."* It was not until Jesus turned 30 that He publicly declared Himself as the Son of God and embarked upon His mission to fulfill the will of the Father. Some may question why He did not reveal Himself earlier, such as at ages 15, 21, or 25. However, it is unlikely that Jesus lacked the ability to communicate His message at those earlier ages, given that His understanding and wisdom had already impressed the teachers of the Law when He was only 12 years old.

That is how the Father God led His Son. In the waiting, Jesus was growing in wisdom and stature. Allow me to repeat it: He was obedient to His earthly authorities, navigating the journey of maturing. In today's modern Christianity, a challenge often emerges when people try to submit to God yet overlook the crucial step of submitting to their earthly leaders and pastors, whom God has carefully appointed to guide and nurture their lives.

God's Way

As you know by now, at the age of 22, I had a supernatural encounter with Jesus Christ. That's when He revealed my calling to me and told me that He would send me all over the earth to spread His fire and anointing. I was ready to go the next day and fulfill my calling. However, years were passing by, and nothing was happening. I was constantly praying that I would do His will. I remained in the Word of God all the time. As a result, I grew in knowledge and understanding. I had testimonies and revelations to share with people, but despite that, I didn't get invited to preach or minister anywhere. I just kept serving in my local church.

One morning, I remember coming to church very early. By then, I was a full-time youth pastor, but I knew that was not what God showed me about my calling. Don't take me wrong; I served in an amazing church and had a fantastic pastor whom I dearly love. He is a precious man of God who has significantly influenced my spiritual growth. Most of all, I am incredibly grateful to my pastor for believing in me and allowing God to lead me. Every month, I would organize youth revival services for the city, and he would attend all of them. It was so encouraging to see him come and be there with us. He would always sit and listen, never interfering with projects, ideas, or service flow. He was just letting God lead me. I am deeply grateful to Pastor Alex for becoming an instrument in God's hands.

Back to the story. It was an early morning, and I came to church before the sun had even risen. I got behind the piano and just began to worship God. That particular morning, I felt His presence in a special way. I was utterly immersed in worship, tears streaming down my face as I praised Him. The only light in the room was a small light bulb in the hallway. I was lost in the moment, playing the piano and worshiping the Lord. At some point, I felt a shift in the atmosphere; it was as if heaven had opened up over me, and then I saw Him—Jesus Himself came into the room and stood beside me. He didn't do or say anything yet. Jesus was just looking at me, and I was overwhelmed with emotion and moved to the side of my chair to offer Jesus a place to sit. And He sat next to me. I continued to play a worship melody in tears while pouring out my heart to Him.

I said, "God, I'm all Yours. I want to be faithful to You. Lead me, I promise to be Your messenger. I promise to be Your mouth. I won't add or withhold anything from Your Word. Let me be Your messenger. You promised that You would send me worldwide to minister to Your people. You promised. And yet, I've been stuck in this city, in these walls, for seven years, and nothing is happening…"

Then, all of a sudden, Jesus placed His hand over my mouth. I felt His palm over my lips. I became silent and could no longer speak.

He began to speak to me, "My son, I've hidden you in this place as a mother hen hides her chicks. I have placed you here to form your character in this slow process. Your time will come very soon. I will lift you up with My own hand. Son, you have no idea how many people will come to destroy you and how many stones will be thrown your way. I am preparing you for everything here in this season. I am raising you to be able to withstand all that is coming and be able to reveal My name to many; continue to trust Me."

I felt ashamed for whining and complaining to God when He said that. Yes, I admit it was in my heart. The next moment, I wholeheartedly submitted myself to the Lord and His ways. I prayed, "Not mine, Your will be done. I am sold out to You. Lead me in Your way. I am all Yours."

The Process of Spiritual Growth

You may have a God-given dream and revelation about your calling and ministry. Remember, it's essential not to go into it ahead of the time set by the Father. Think of it as a season in which He develops you and builds your character. Do not rush this vital process or attempt to "help" God in terms of reaching your calling. By the way, I am not suggesting you be as passive as possible. I just want to highlight the ways of God, His methods, and principles. You are not alone in this season. He is with you. He watches your growth and cultivates you to bring you to maturity so you can fulfill His will.

Perhaps you have reached a certain level of knowledge of God and dedication to Him, but you have not yet passed the process of growth.

While in it, you will learn to deny certain things, to control your reactions, and to make your decisions consciously. You might find yourself at a crossroads, where one side is the opinion of God and on the other are opinions of good, successful, and influential people. And each time, you must decide whether to submit to men's opinions or accept God's ways. This won't be easy.

When the Holy Spirit begins to lead you, He leads you on a narrow path. This is where God gets up close and personal with you, leaving no room for anyone else. That's why the path is narrow: it's your own journey with God. On this path, you will die to yourself to allow God to bring you through the process of adoption. There, you will come to your senses. There, you will kill your ego, and there, you will bury reliance on the opinion of man, along with every form of fear, pride, and hypocrisy. There, all the uneven and crooked ways will be made straight so that the glory of the Lord can be revealed in your life.

God cares so much about you as His child, and that's why He leads you in His ways. Yield to the guidance of the Holy Spirit. Allow Him to deal with your heart. And remember, all who are led by the Spirit of God are sons of God.

God's Voice in Your Life

God has never intended for us to remain spiritual babies. He wants us to move forward into transformation, adoption, and maturity in Him. While we are spiritually maturing, we depend on the voice of God all the time. However, when we enter into sonship, we begin to understand how the Father thinks, so we don't always have to ask questions. Let me explain. When children grow, they depend entirely on the parents' voice to guide and teach basic things: don't go there, don't touch this, etc. As children mature and reach adulthood, their reliance on their parents' voice diminishes, and their own way of thinking develops. Consequently, a grown-up child often understands what the father wants without having to ask.

Today, we have so many sermons and books available to us on how to hear the voice of God and how God speaks. Although these are good messages in which believers share their experiences and different methods or strategies to hear God, I want to go back to the basics. See, **if God spoke to everyone the same way, we would not need to have a personal relationship with Him.** That's why we should focus less on forms and methods of the way He speaks and instead focus more on getting closer to God and becoming one with Him so we can start thinking like Him and know His ways.

Unfortunately, many believers are hesitant to grow spiritually and instead rely on external voices; they often say things like, "I need to go to a prophet and ask God," or "I'll just pray with the prophet and do what he tells me. To move or not to move? To buy or not to buy? To get married or not?" Despite being long-time Christians, these individuals struggle to mature and still depend on someone else's relationship with God, whether a pastor or someone else. I believe the time has come for the Church to grow in sonship, start thinking as the Father does, and begin to do His will.

I wholeheartedly believe that having the mind of Christ and His way of thinking is the highest possible level of hearing God's voice. Let this truth soak into you. Then, we will no longer wait for the activations, prophets, or signs, but we will know what to do, when to do it, and how to respond in various situations.

The highest level of hearing God's voice is when we attain the mind of Christ: when we start to understand and perceive things just as the Father does.

I noticed that some believers, over time, might develop a fear that if God does not say anything to them, they are doing something wrong. However, it's important to remember that this is not necessarily the case. Have you ever used a GPS while driving? You are going in the right direction when the navigation system is silent. It will not be repeating the same command every 5 minutes. But if you go off course or a turn is coming, the GPS begins to voice the directions to get you back on track to the set destination. That's why if God is silent, chances are, you are on the right path. Keep going! If you are on the cleaning crew in your church and God isn't saying anything yet, keep cleaning; this means you are on the right track. Keep seeking God's face and be in His presence; when it's time to make a turn, you will know and hear His voice. God will speak to you in a way where you won't miss it!

Allow the Holy Spirit to Lead You

Allow the Holy Spirit to lead you. I don't know what kind of church you attend, but please don't allow these thoughts to cross your mind, "Oh man, my pastor is not spiritual enough. If only I had a pastor like pastor Andrey." Listen, God has already sent me into your life through this book, and you can learn and go deeper with God. However, it's not about me. I believe you need a pastor in your local church to mature you in some areas of your life that God is currently working on. Remember, He uses pastors, leaders, and sometimes even people who may not be overtly spiritual to help you shed the burdens of pride, hypocrisy, and other undesirable junk that God is not pleased with. Stay faithful where you are; do not grumble; do not blame anyone; do not try to prove anything to anyone; do not try to exalt yourself over others; do not attempt to appear super spiritual. Let people read your life. Let your transformed mindset and inner character speak louder than your words. And when they ask you questions, show them the way to the Father.

Also, please do not be quick to tell people they are doing things wrong. I hear the Lord saying to many of you now, *What is that to you? You follow Me.*

I pray that you will follow God's path; it is my deepest desire. Sometimes, it may feel like His process is way too slow, but that's what it takes to form a godly character within you. Allow the Holy Spirit to lead you. Keep going. Be a blessing to the people around you. Be a blessing to your pastors and leaders. Pray for them. I am sure they are good people. Remember, God is leading you. It's your own narrow path. And God will raise you in due time and guide you into doing His will. If you feel you are in the process of growing and maturing right now, I pray that God will help you make the right decisions and not rush ahead of Him.

The Spirit of the LORD is Upon Me

From the time spanning from Luke 2:52, when Jesus was still a teenager, to Luke 4:18, when He boldly declared in the synagogue, *"... the Spirit of the LORD is upon Me..." This* was a significant period in His life, where He flourished and matured as the Son. Yes, Jesus needed this growth period—not just physical growth, but maturity in God, the Son of Man, growing in the Father's house under His lordship.

When the fullness of time came, Jesus revealed Himself to Israel proclaiming these words, *"The Spirit of the LORD is upon Me"* (Luke

4:18). Note that He didn't say, "'The Holy Spirit is upon Me," but "the **Spirit of the LORD** is upon Me." In the previous chapter, we discussed what the lordship of God means. Therefore, you know the difference between you having the Holy Spirit and the Holy Spirit having you and becoming the Lord of your life. And when He becomes the Lord of your life, He anoints you to fulfill His will. The connection between the anointing of the Holy Spirit and the fulfillment of the Father's will is inseparable from His lordship.

As the congregation gathered in the synagogue, Jesus rose to His feet to read. He opened the book of the prophet Isaiah, found this passage of Scripture, and began to read:

> *The Spirit of the LORD is upon Me because He has anointed Me to preach the gospel to the poor; He has sent Me to heal the brokenhearted, to proclaim liberty to the captives and recovery of sight to the blind, to set at liberty those who are oppressed; to proclaim the acceptable year of the LORD (Luke 4:18-19).*

Jesus intentionally hand-picked a specific part of the book of Isaiah to read. As He began reading, the words resonated with Him, but before reaching the end of the prophecy, Jesus gently closed the book. Why did He do that? The reason lies in the nature of the prophecy itself, which is connected to the Cross and the fact that Jesus would save, deliver, heal, and restore humanity. The second part of the prophecy refers to what would come after the Cross; that is why Jesus stopped where He did. On one side of the Cross, He proclaims the good news to the poor. On the other side, He proclaims to those in Zion who have already experienced the transformative power of His salvation. What is His proclamation? Let's read the other part of that prophecy from the book of Isaiah:

> *To console those who mourn in Zion, to give them beauty for ashes, the oil of joy for mourning, The garment of praise for the spirit of heaviness; That they may be called trees of righteousness, The planting of the LORD, that He may be glorified (Isaiah 61:3).*

Isaiah prophesied enlightenment, redemption, a crown of beauty, oil of gladness, and glorious garments of praise. In other words, he is prophesying the restoration of sonship! That's what happened on the other side of the Cross. We encountered these same elements in the parable of the prodigal son, which we discussed in the previous chapters. And then, when sonship is restored, we come to an understanding of why God gave it to us in the first place:

> *And they shall rebuild the old ruins, they shall raise up the former desolations, and they shall repair the ruined cities, the desolations of many generations (Isaiah 61:4).*

This passage of Scripture has a profound meaning—with the restoration of sons and daughters of God, the process of all creation is being restored. And the earth will be filled with the glory of God through His sons and daughters.

Growing in sonship involves submitting to the lordship of God in your life. Again, I'm not talking about growing in ministry but growing in sonship, coming to know God as *LORD*, and fully submitting to Him.

Father and Son

As I've mentioned before, the concept of Father and Son is essential for your spiritual growth. Jesus perfectly modeled what this relationship with the Father should look like.

Let's take a look at the following Bible verses:

I and My Father are one (John 10:30),

He who has seen Me has seen the Father (John 14:9).

…I am in the Father, and the Father in Me… The words that I speak to you I do not speak on My own authority; but the Father who dwells in Me does the works (John 14:10).

All things have been delivered to Me by My Father, and no one knows the Son except the Father. Nor does anyone know the Father except the Son, and the one to whom the Son will reveal Him (Matthew 11:27).

These Scriptures clearly say that the emphasis should not be on ministry growth but on the growth of sonship. I am talking about a profound connection with the Father and a passion to know Him and fulfill His will. Let me give you an example: Many people know me as a pastor, minister, author, musician, and friend, but none know me as a father. Only son, born of me, whom I raised, taught, cared for, and played with, knows me as a father. He is always in contact with me, learning from me, growing up under my roof. Other people don't know me as a father because they are not a part of my family and don't live in my house. It's a different type of relationship and a greater level of intimacy.

Therefore, our assignment is to grow in sonship and maturity. People often ask me, "How do you practically grow up and mature in sonship?" The answer is simple—you won't be able to grow in sonship without coming to know the Father. The opposite is also true: You cannot come to know the Father and not grow in sonship. The close, intimate relationship with Him will become the catalyst and mechanism to trigger your transformation process. And when you begin to see the Father doing, you won't be able to remain passive; your ministry will find you.

Learn from Me

Jesus' life on earth was a true embodiment of a close relationship with the Father. I'm grateful for the example that He set for us. He didn't just preach. He also said, "Learn from Me" (see Matthew 11:29). Friend, do you want to learn from Him? Or only listen to the good things He says? Jesus was surrounded by many people who were listening attentively, yet there were those who remained unchanged. Among them was Judas, a member of Jesus' ministry who never transformed and submitted to His lordship. Do not make the same mistake as those people did: your ministry should not be the place of your intimacy with God, nor should it be a place of your intimate worship unto God, and the ministry should definitely never replace the process of personal transformation. Ministry should never become your goal. The goal should always be to know Him and to fulfill God's will through the ministry.

Let's delve into the model of Jesus' relationship with His Father.

First, in the example Jesus set for us, we see He only went into ministry once the Spirit of the Lord had all of Him.

Second, Jesus' attention was not on the ministry but on the Father and His will.

Have a look at how Jesus' ministry was unfolding:

> *However, the report went around concerning **Him** all the more; and great multitudes came together to hear, and to be healed by **Him** of their infirmities (Luke 5:15).*

Note the phrases "the report concerning Him," and "come to hear Him," "to be healed by Him." It is fascinating that while people's attention was on Jesus, all of His attention was on His Father.

Imagine a world where the testimonies and stories about Jesus spread like wildfire. In today's modern era, it would be as if news about Him went viral throughout all social media platforms: Instagram, Facebook, TikTok, YouTube, etc. Jesus was the talk of town: "There's this young rabbi. He's in His early thirties, causing a stir with mind-boggling miracles. His ministry is a hub of healing where people find relief from all kinds of sickness and disease. But that's not all: He has unparalleled authority over demons, and they obey Him and flee. He does unimaginable things science can't explain: signs, miracles, and wonders are everyday occurrences around Him. He doesn't preach like scribes or Pharisees. He fed thousands of people with only five loaves and two fish. He resurrected the widow's son from the dead. Is He the Messiah we've all been waiting for...?"

The news about Jesus spread all the more. People wanted to come and get healed of their sicknesses. The more the word spread about Him, the more the people came to Him. So many ministries are seeking this type of fame today. After all, isn't this the revival we should all be waiting for? It is awesome! Everyone talks about you; everyone comes to you.

Do you know that the more people come to you, the busier you are with ministry? Here's the catch: the more people talk about you, and the more your ministry expands, the more chances that your self-esteem, ego, and pride will increase with it.

Let's take a moment to reflect on the impact of Jesus in Israel. People flocked to Him everywhere He went, eager to listen to Him and experience His healing power. Jesus captured the attention of all who crossed His path; it's no wonder His fame spread far and wide. And here is what Jesus did:

So He Himself often withdrew into the wilderness and prayed (Luke 5:16).

Some disciples might question, "Jesus, why are you leaving? Look how many people come to you! Such a success! They need Your ministry. There are better times to go and pray. After all, You are fulfilling the will of God. Why would you leave all these people?"

Yes, people kept coming to Jesus. However, He wasn't there to build His own ministry but to fulfill the will of the Father. You may ask, "But isn't that the same thing? Isn't the Father's will to serve as many people as possible?"

The difference between doing ministry and doing the will of the Father is determined **by what your attention is on.**

Let me emphasize. When Jesus retreated to the wilderness, it was not to intercede for His ministry or prepare messages. His purpose was not to seek more anointing or increase God's power upon His life. Revivals, provisions, or signs from above were not His focus. Jesus didn't leave to vent His feelings to God, either. Instead, He chose to pause. This is a significant decision. He stopped all the busyness and hassle and entered the rest of God. He would withdraw to be with the Father and see the Father doing—a unique and profound experience.

I pray you would have a moment of epiphany as I did—Jesus was captivated not by the ministry but by the Father. That's why it was a priority for Him to leave the ministry behind to spend time with the Father.

For you to fulfill God's will, your attention should be on God, not on the ministry.

Have you ever considered what Jesus' time with the Father looked like? Have you thought about what Jesus prayed about? There are different kinds of prayers: Thanksgiving, intercession, supplication, petition, proclamation, etc. These are all good forms of prayer; each has its own place and time. But there is another type of prayer: the secret place of the

Almighty, where there is no room for anything or anyone else, just you and God. There, you speak less and listen more. You present yourself to the Lord so He will speak to you there.

Interestingly, Jesus didn't persuade or force His disciples to pray more. He didn't teach a lot about prayer. He would just withdraw to solitary places to pray. This simple act of devotion caught His disciples' attention so much that they came to Jesus themselves and asked Him, *"Lord, teach us to pray, as John also taught his disciples"* (Luke 11:1).

Jesus' Secret Place

In chapter 5 of his book, the apostle John unveils an interesting insight into Jesus' secret place. There, we see the unity and coherence between the Father and the Son:

> *But Jesus answered them, "My Father has been working until now, and I have been working." Therefore the Jews sought all the more to kill Him, because He not only broke the Sabbath, but also said that God was His Father, making Himself equal with God. Then Jesus answered and said to them, "Most assuredly, I say to you, the Son can do nothing of Himself, but what He sees the Father do; for whatever He does, the Son also does in like" (John 5:17-19).*

These verses reveal the secret place of Jesus, His connection, unity with God, and devotion to the Father. The Son willingly submits to the Father. This is the highest level of freedom: total dependence on the Lord.

Ironically, Jesus' unity with the Father exasperated the religious people. They were irritated by Him doing the works of God because it would interfere with their planned services, traditions, rituals, and programs.

They were angry by Him calling God His Father. They were enraged by Him making Himself equal to God. However, that only testified about Jesus' relationship with the Father.

We just read, "The Son can do nothing of Himself." Technically, He could and would have no problem doing things of Himself. He definitely could have done a lot. He could've started His own ministry at 12 and been popular. However, the phrase *can do nothing of Himself* demonstrates His obedience and level of dedication to the Father, as well as His maturity, sonship, and unity with the Father.

Before Jesus came to this world, before the Word became flesh, He said, "*Behold, I have come to do Your will*" (Hebrews 10:7). This is a crucial moment. He didn't say: "I know what needs to be done." Not at all. Instead, He proclaims: "I have come to do Your will." The Son willingly submits to the Father. That's why He says, "The Son can do nothing of Himself." Just think logically about it: Could He do things of Himself? Absolutely, He proved this in the Garden of Gethsemane. When the soldiers came to arrest Jesus, He said, "If I wanted to, I could call more than 12 legions of angels, and they would have destroyed everything here." But He didn't. That makes the difference. Jesus wasn't fulfilling His own plans. Jesus wasn't building His own ministry. He wasn't acting according to His own discretion.

Jesus was doing the will of the Father. In the Garden of Gethsemane, He prayed, "Not My will, but Your will be done, here on earth as it is in heaven." He submitted His will, choices, and life to the Father.

The apostle Paul also recognizes this model:

> *I beseech you therefore, brethren, by the mercies of God, that you present your bodies a living sacrifice, holy, acceptable to God, which is your reasonable service. And do not be conformed to this world, but be transformed by the renewing*

> *of your mind, that you may prove what is that good and acceptable and perfect will of God (Romans 12:1-2).*

We also need to learn to present ourselves fully to the Father so that when (or if) we enter into ministry, it will not captivate us fully or become our god, but that we withdraw from ministry and see what the Father is doing.

Think about it, where is your attention now? "The Son can do nothing of His own accord, but only what He sees the Father doing. For the Father loves the Son and shows Him all He does…" —this should be the core of our secret place. When that is in order, everything else falls into its place. Thus, a secret place is not a form of prayer but the state of your focus, mind, and heart. You desire to set time apart to be with God and present yourself to the Lord so He would reveal Himself. He would speak and share His heart with you there.

Jesus is speaking to you today, "I have revealed and demonstrated this model of the secret place to you—I have lived it out with My Father. Learn from Me, and you will be able to continue doing what I did, even greater than I did. The same Spirit that was in Me dwells in you, and He will enable you to live your life exactly the way I did. You can live in a close relationship with the Father, just like Me. Don't just fill yourself with the information I teach you. Learn from Me, and you will be able to continue what I started".

From this chapter forward, I welcome you to the incredible process of diving into the secret place, under His lordship, and into the Holy of Holies.

Chapter 5
What Was That?

> *Blessed are the poor in spirit, for theirs is the kingdom of heaven.*
>
> *Matthew 5:3*

It so happened that after I surrendered my life to God, I became friends with an incredible elderly lady, who lived nearby. Fondly, I referred to her as grandma. She was fully devoted to God and taught me how to pray, cast out demons, declare the Word of God, and hear the voice of the Holy Spirit. Often, after work, I stopped by her house, and we prayed together. All I can say is that she was on fire for God. I am so grateful for elder Christians who don't judge the younger generation but instead choose to intercede for them, offering support, encouragement, and, most importantly, proclaiming the promises of God into their lives. That's precisely how this grandma was; she never judged me, even when I stumbled and made mistakes. She was just like the prophetess Anna mentioned in the Gospel of Luke 2:36. The Bible says Anna reached a very old age and did not leave the Temple, serving God day and night with fasting and prayer (Luke 2:37). Note that she was called a prophetess who served God with prayer. *Why was a woman serving God with a prayer called a prophet? What does it mean?* To prophesy in prayer is not about predicting the future; it is not to reveal the sins of young people, and it is not to frighten people with the judgment of God. To prophesy in prayer is to proclaim the Word of God and His will into peoples' lives, futures, situations, circumstances, and this generation.

Prayer and the Word

God started teaching me this through His Word. In Psalm 103:19-22, it is written:

> *The LORD has established His throne in heaven, and His kingdom rules over all.*
>
> *Bless the LORD, you His angels, who excel in strength, who do His word, heeding the voice of His word.*
>
> *Bless the LORD, all you His hosts, you [a]ministers of His, who do His pleasure.*
>
> *Bless the LORD, all His works, in all places of His dominion.*
>
> *Bless the LORD, O my soul!*

Through this passage of Scripture, we can recognize the structure of God's Kingdom and how it operates:

First, the throne of the LORD stands supreme above all else.

Second, around His throne are His mighty angels, who excel in strength. As we all know, there are different ranks and kinds of angels, but this kind of angel is endowed with the power to carry out/fulfill God's

Word when it is voiced. Their full attention and focus are directed to complete this assignment. When the servants of God (sons) speak His Word on earth, the heavenly hosts (angels) that operate between heaven and earth begin to act in accordance with their function.

Therefore, the Word of God must first be voiced on earth for the angels to start fulfilling it. Those angels heed the voice of His Word. This voice is the Word-based prayers coming from the mouths of intercessors, God's servants, and His holy people. It is crucial to emphasize that we, as God's representatives on this earth, are responsible for speaking the Word of God with our lips.

Sometimes, it seems to me that a lot of angels in heaven are sitting idle because God's people on earth keep praying only about their problems, describing emotions, situations, feelings of how hard it is for them, etc. Many people get caught up in their emotions and only pray to God to vent to Him; they talk and rant and then leave. Please don't assume that the more you talk in prayer, the more God will pay attention to you. For it is written:

> *And when you pray, do not use vain repetitions as the heathen do. For they think that they will be heard for their many words (Matthew 6:7).*

Sometimes, when I witness people praying, their words flow with eloquence and beauty that it touches the soul, causing a whirlwind of emotions, and you find yourself at the verge of tears. It seems to listeners that God has to answer this kind of prayer. But angels are not impressed with those beautiful expressions, tears, emotions, or eloquent speeches. The mighty angels near the throne respond to fulfill God's Word, not our pleading. They respond to God's Word coming from our mouths.

While in prayer, shift your focus from your feelings to your identity as a child of God, understand your position as God's son/daughter, stop whining and venting, and start voicing out what is written—Scripture and God's promises—you will see a decisive shift in the spiritual realm, where heaven begins to move. Let me repeat it: Angels react to and obey the voice of His Word in your mouth and fulfill what is written.

Intercessory Prayer

Intercession is one of the most powerful types of prayer. We see this kind of prayer highlighted throughout the Bible. Interestingly, Abraham, Moses, David, and other prophets were intercessors. Moreover, the Lord Jesus interceded for His disciples and everyone who will believe in Him through their words (see John 17). *Why is intercessory prayer so important?* There are things we can't see with our physical eyes, but the spiritual realm can see them. God once showed me a place in Scripture that explains what happens in the spiritual realm when intercessory prayers are over a person's life. The book of Job records a conversation between God and satan, where the devil says to the Lord:

> *"Have You not made a hedge around him, around his household, and around all that he has on every side? You have blessed the work of his hands, and his possessions have increased in the land"* (Job 1:10).

Isn't that fascinating? The adversary sees what we don't: *a hedge around him.* It means that in the spiritual realm, God sets a hedge or a wall of protection around us, our families, our possessions, and the works of our hands. Satan sees this hedge of protection and becomes utterly helpless in the face of it.

I personally believe intercessory prayer creates a powerful hedge around a person's life, preventing satan from getting in. The enemy becomes powerless when seeing and recognizing this hedge. Let me remind you of what I mentioned earlier: For intercessory prayer to have an impact, it must be founded on Scripture and aligned with God's will. When we build this wall of prayer, the angels of God watch over the Word that was voiced to fulfill it.

A Grandma in the Temple

In the book of Luke, it says:

> *There was also a prophet, Anna, the daughter of Penuel, of the tribe of Asher. She was very old; she had lived with her husband seven years after her marriage, and then was a widow until she was eighty-four. She never left the temple but worshiped night and day, fasting and praying (Luke 2:36-37 NIV).*

This blessed woman of God was a mighty prayer warrior, and her ministry of intercession was marked with prophecy. In other words, she was filled with the Holy Spirit and declared the Word of God in her prayers—that was how she served God day and night. Intercessory prayer must be prophetic. I cannot stress enough how crucial it is to understand this concept: To prophesy in prayer is to declare the Word of God into a person's life, situations, circumstances, and into our generation, just like Anna did in her lifetime. Anna would proclaim the Word of God day and night, and the heavens responded to her Scripture-based prayers. I believe that because of her unwavering faithfulness in this ministry, God added years to her life and allowed her to see His salvation: the promised birth of the Messiah. That is a powerful testament to her devotion.

So, dear grandmas, we need your prayers and your ministry of intercession before God. It releases God's power into our generation! Only with your support will we be able to fulfill the will of God and see His glory manifest, each in obedience to their own ministry and calling. I am deeply grateful to those who are already praying for us. May God enable you to taste and see the fruit of this ministry, and may you see His glory and salvation manifest in this generation!

Prayer in the Spirit

And so, one day, when I was talking with "my" grandma, she said, "Andrey, you should pray more in the Spirit. It will build you from within and help you stay on fire for God. And when you burn for God, it will be easier for the Holy Spirit to lead you. So, pray in tongues a lot!"

I started doing that. Back then, I had a job as a delivery driver. Most of the day, I was driving alone in my vehicle and had a lot of time to pray in tongues on the road. I would pray in the Spirit at home, too, but my job allowed me to take that to the next level.

Through my years of ministry, I learned different types of prayer and practiced all of them. It wouldn't be right to say that one form of prayer is better than the others. However, here is what I realized about **praying in tongues—it serves as an open door to another dimension.** Praying in the Spirit is a mighty spiritual weapon given to God's people; it helps lead you into the will of the God for your life. Here is what the apostle Paul says about it:

> *Likewise the Spirit also helps in our weaknesses. For we do not know what we should pray for as we ought, but the Spirit Himself makes intercession for us with groanings*

which cannot be uttered. Now He who searches the hearts knows what the mind of the Spirit is, because He makes intercession for the saints according to the will of God (Romans 8:26-27).

Understand that when you pray in the Spirit, you intercede in accordance with the perfect will of God. The Spirit of God directs such prayer. Thus, it carries God's thoughts, which He can reveal to you while you pray. That's why it's essential to stay focused even during prayer in tongues and not turn your brain off and let your thoughts wander while automatically speaking in tongues.

For example, while praying in tongues, fully immerse yourself in prayer and try to be sensitive, listening to your spirit. Remember, your spirit is connected with the Holy Spirit. He is interceding for something or someone and can reveal it to you. I pay attention to the tone and direction of my prayer in tongues and ask the Holy Spirit to give me an understanding of what I am interceding for at the moment. After all, prayer in tongues is the Father's language; it carries His thoughts, and I want to understand them so I can also pray with my words and declare the Word of God into those situations. Apostle Paul writes: *"So what shall I do? I will pray with my spirit, but I will also pray with my understanding"* (1 Corinthians 14:15*)*. Both are equally important.

I don't let my mind wander when praying in the Spirit. I focus on God, immersing myself in His presence, and begin recognizing and following the Spirit's leading and promptings. Often, I begin to see things in the Spirit. I can feel it when my spirit intercedes for my future or situations. Sometimes, I begin to see someone's face and understand that the Holy Spirit is interceding for them. Sometimes, my spiritual tongues change, and when I see another country and people there, I know that I'm interceding for them. That's why I said praying in the Spirit is a door to a different dimension. You may have experienced it, too.

At the same time, a thought can come: Why pray for something else that is irrelevant to you? The devil or even your mind will try to confuse you and urge you to pray for your own needs, *You have enough of your own problems. Why waste time praying for someone? Why pray for other countries or someone's situation?* Do not judge according to the flesh; be sensitive to the leading of the Holy Spirit. I believe those are special moments with God when He seeks and finds a person who can intercede according to His will and declare His word in a particular situation. Obey His prompting, and He will take care of your needs supernaturally.

Have you ever attended a prayer meeting where you've been given a list of needs, and everyone would jump into intercession? There is a better and more effective way of intercession. If only we would take the time to first enter into His presence with praise and thanksgiving, to connect with God, so He could intercede through us and direct our prayers, then intercession would carry God's power and not feel like a burden. That way, we would enjoy prayer meetings even when we engage in spiritual warfare.

Friend, to summarize, be focused and sensitive when you pray in tongues. Prayer in the Spirit is intercession in agreement with the will of God. Furthermore, when we add prayer with understanding and declare the Scripture that the Spirit places into our hearts, we become a prophetic voice, speaking the will of God.

Prophetic Prayer and the Word

Here's the dilemma: If we don't know the Word of God, we can't use it in prayer, and the Holy Spirit won't be able to remind us of the Word when we need it. Therefore, we absolutely need to know and memorize the Scriptures. God often speaks using His Word. I experience it all the time. Scriptures emerge from within when I pray, which means that the Holy Spirit wants me to speak them. He knows what I have memorized, and I don't need time to search for them to declare them. The more time I spend in the Word of God, the more my prayers gradually align with the Word and influence my walk with God.

Here is what I want to highlight—it's essential for us to memorize the Scripture. That way, the Holy Spirit becomes a manager or a conductor for these verses and brings them up when we pray. When I declare His Word in prayer, I begin to feel His authority and anointing and see how things shift in the spiritual realm.

Honestly, I've never sat down and worked on memorizing Bible verses. I just spend a lot of time, and I mean A LOT, reading and meditating on the Word of God. The Word has become a part of me to the point where I can cite entire chapters. I've never tried memorizing Bible verses by heart; I just read them over and over and meditated on them a lot.

If you find it challenging to remember Scripture, look for ways that will help you memorize it. Choose the method that suits you. For example, there are some phone apps available today that you might find helpful. The main thing is that you do it and grow in knowing the Word.

Why at Night?

To be honest, I get selfish when it comes to getting to know God. I often say, "God, I don't know about other people, but I want to know You more. I am hungry for more of You. Don't look for anyone else; You've found me. Lord, take me and use me." I have said this multiple times, both to myself and to God.

And so, one day at work, as I was praying in tongues, a thought suddenly came to me, *Set your alarm clock for 3 a.m. and get up to spend time with God.* That thought was unexpected: waking up in the middle of the night, not to pray or intercede, but just to be with God. I had no clue what that should look like, but I was in for it.

So, while setting my alarm clock that evening, I was thinking, "Andrey, what are you doing? You always go to bed late and wake up early to go to work. Why get up at 3 a.m. when you don't get enough sleep in the first place? Are you sure you heard it from God? You pray morning and night and all day at work. Why do you need to also get up in the middle of the night to be with God?" Despite all these thoughts, I believed the Holy Spirit inspired that idea, so I didn't consult my feelings or my logic and did it anyway.

I still remember that first night. The alarm went off, and I started battling my flesh. At last, I managed to get up and spend time with God. I kept doing it every night since then for weeks and months. I was being persistent. I wanted to know Him. Time passed, and all my excitement and feelings were gone, but what remained was my firm decision to continue growing in God and being with Him. Soon enough, I no longer needed an alarm clock; my body adjusted, and I would get up without it. There were also some nights when the Holy Spirit would wake me up.

Back then, we rented a small apartment where the living room and the kitchen were open-concept. There was a TV between those rooms and a little space next to it in the corner. We had only one TV channel working with a clear picture, TBN. The rest of the channels were blurry. Some evenings, I would just sit in the corner and watch Benny Hinn's services on TBN, worshipping God along with him.

I would come to the same corner between the kitchen and living room at night. I would kneel and worship Him for half an hour. During those 30 minutes, I would not pray for needs, just worship. I would say, "God, look! Everyone is asleep, and I'm not. I am so hungry for You. Draw me closer to You. Reveal Yourself to me. I love You so much. I am not asking for anything. I'm just here to be with You…" Sometimes, I would worship God, and sometimes I would remain silent and wait for Him. I would focus and keep all my attention on Him. That's how I would spend my 30 minutes with God at night before going back to bed. To some of you, this may seem silly, but it was my heart's desire and sincerity.

What Was That?

One night, I got up as usual and went to the same corner where I would usually pray, but I first wanted to go to the kitchen to drink some water to wake myself up. When I stepped into the place where I typically kneel to pray, I was struck by a high-voltage electric current. I fell down and immediately started to shake. "What was that?"—I asked myself, lying on the floor. I forgot where I was going. Such fear came over me that I immediately began praying in tongues. I did not understand what just happened.

When I finally calmed down and my thoughts became silent, I heard the voice of God saying, *"Son, this is the place I wait for you every night. The moment you decided to get up at 3 a.m. for Me, just* **to be with Me**—*I sanctified this place and time for Myself. I wait for you here every night."*

Whoa! I realized that God longs for our presence more than we long for His. I realized God is not busy; it is us. I realized that people waited for God in the Old Testament, but in the New Testament, God is waiting for us. He was the One who initiated a relationship with humanity; He loved us before we loved Him.

I was on my knees, in great awe and silence before the Lord, and I heard Him say, *"If you really want to get to know Me, extend this time in your life."*

The next day, I could only pray in the Spirit and think about what happened at night. "Wow! How can you explain that? I used to pray for 3 hours straight, I've never been hit like that. Why did God respond to that prayer more than anything else? How were that half an hour different from all my other prayers? Why did those 30 minutes touch God's heart so much? It wasn't my intercession, praying in tongues all day, or declarations that evoked that response; it was that half hour every night." I will never forget that moment at night.

Don't Try to Relive Someone Else's Experience

The year following my first encounter with Jesus, I had several spiritual experiences. And I still have them. I don't talk about them often, and it's not because those experiences aren't significant. They are. I chose not to talk about them because people want to hear someone else's experience more than to build their relationship with God and have their own experience with Him. You can't copy and paste mine or Benny Hinn's walk with God into your life; that would be like trying to recreate a masterpiece. I've tried waking up and saying, "Good morning, Holy Spirit," like Benny Hinn did, but it wasn't working for me. Nothing happened. I had to develop and cultivate my own relationship with God, not recreate his.

I am sharing these moments I had with God only to show you the principles God used to lead me closer to Him. I am not trying to encourage you to copy my walk with God or style of prayer. I want to help you understand that God always has more—there is always something more profound, higher, and greater than what you already see and know about Him. When we get that, we ignite our zeal for God. Learn from my shared truths and experiences, but build your own relationship with God. Your relationship with Him won't be like someone else's; you need your own experience with God. It is a personal path to walk.

The Secret Place

The next night, you can't even imagine how carefully I approached that corner. I tried my best to go around that spot to get some water and was very cautious about getting on my knees.

I couldn't help but wonder about that night. Why did those 30 minutes move His heart?

1. Desire

First of all, it was my strong desire and hunger for God. I wanted to get to know Him and have intimacy with Him. This hunger gave me strength to get up in the middle of the night. I must remind you that I would not ask God for anything during that time except to reveal Himself to me. I wasn't seeking God because of my needs, and trust me, I had plenty of them. I got up because I wanted to have a closer relationship with Him, and that touched God's heart.

When building a relationship with God, you need to work on discipline. After establishing spiritual discipline and doing this consistently for a long time, you will need to ask God for hunger. Hunger for God is something that only the Holy Spirit Himself can place in you. Therefore, in the beginning, discipline yourself, then in the process, fight for hunger, cultivate it, and pray for it. Ask, and it will be given to you.

2. Environment

Secondly, I was in a peaceful environment. Subconsciously, my mind understood it was nighttime. Everyone and everything was asleep. No distractions. All the busyness around me stopped. No hassle. No commotion. I wasn't in a hurry. My entire surrounding was still and silent. When I prayed during the daytime, noises and distractions were always in the way, diverting my focus. Daytime tasks, situations, needs, text messages, and many other things demanded my attention, so my thoughts would go to those things, situations, or circumstances. Nighttime would be the complete opposite experience. It was a time when everything would stop, and my mind could be at peace and rest.

I encourage you to refrain from copying my exact prayer schedule. Some people prefer to get up early in the morning to pray. If that's you, keep doing that. Spend time with God in the morning when you can focus on Him. Some people might struggle to wake up early. That's fine, too. You're not a morning person; do it when you can. Some pray in the evening, and others during the day. The most important thing is to set that time apart for God and make sure that it's quality time. Keep developing and cultivating your relationship with Him and building your secret place.

3. Sacrifice

Considering my hectic schedule, those 30 minutes at night were a **huge** sacrifice. But I decided to give up my sleep and comfort for one goal—to be with God and get to know Him closely. Yes, at times, I felt exhausted. I went to bed late, woke up early, worked full-time, was involved in church ministry, hosted a small group, and had family responsibilities. However, I was happy to do this for Him alone, without being noticed by man. I wanted God to see me and accept this sacrifice. I sacrificed my precious sleep for time with God, offering myself without grumbling or complaining, with great hunger and determination to know Him. This was the sacrifice **the Holy Spirit led me to.** I kept pressing in. The day I experienced God's "electric" current was about a year after I started doing this. Following that experience, I continued doing this for a few more years.

4. Attention

When something is valuable to you, all your attention is there, including your thoughts, hearts, and desires. When this costs you a lot, you perceive it differently. That is why, during those 30 minutes, all my attention was on God. I focused my heart on Him so He would have all of me. Let me emphasize that I was there for Him alone, period, and that's why I could put all my focus and attention on Him.

God, What Should I Do?

This chapter has discussed different kinds of prayer: Intercession, praying in the Spirit, prophetic prayer, and the secret place. All types of prayer are important in your walk with God. All these types of prayer are also interconnected.

I believe that prayer in tongues is what led me to spend time with God at night. The thought came from the Holy Spirit as I was praying, and I accepted it. He was interceding to take me deeper in my relationship with Himself. He was the One who initiated and prompted this notion.

The Holy Spirit works in you to bring you back to the Father's will under the lordship of Christ. Therefore, pray in tongues a lot. When you pray in the Spirit, focus on your tongues, and you will comprehend what your spirit is praying about. Then you can pray with understanding, too, and declare the Scriptures.

Remember that your mission and the mission of angels are intertwined. We are to be God's voice on earth and declare His Word in prayer. Then, the angels who excel in strength begin to function and carry out God's spoken Word.

Many believers pray, intercede, and experience God's presence but don't have the habit of coming to God just to be with Him. The secret place is different from a prayer closet. The secret place is your close relationship with God, where you present yourself entirely as a living sacrifice and set the conditions—the place, time, and atmosphere. There, you make sure that nothing distracts you so that you can enter into His rest, connect with God, and hear Him.

I thought I had reached new heights with God, but there is always something bigger, further, wider, higher, and deeper in Him. The Holy Spirit began to lead me even further. God spoke to me again, "Extend this time."

I, again, needed help understanding how to do that. I began to pray in the Spirit again and listen to where God wanted to lead me. *God, what should I do? How can I extend this time? I don't understand...* Suddenly, the Word began to speak to me. I started seeing places in Scripture get highlighted to me. I saw that when God set Moses apart for Himself, He called him to go to the mountain to be with Him. I saw Abraham, David, and Elijah. I saw Jesus, Peter, James, and John, who ascended the Mount of Transfiguration to be with God. There, they had such powerful experiences and revelations of God that they otherwise wouldn't have if they stayed down below with everyone else. Wait a minute. Why a mountain?

I stopped and asked: "God, do you actually want me to..."

And as if from eternity itself, I heard His voice calling me, *"Come out of the camp, ascend to the mountain, and stand before My face."*

Chapter 6
Teach Me, Holy Spirit!

Be still, and know that I am God! I will be honored by every nation. I will be honored throughout the world.

Psalm 46:10 NLT

In the gospel writings, Peter, James, and John were always by Jesus' side. You may have noticed that wherever Jesus was, these three disciples were there with Him. For example, when Jesus visited Jairus' house, Peter, James, and John went in with Him. When Jesus went up on the mountain of Transfiguration, Peter, James, and John followed Him and beheld His glory. These three disciples clung to Jesus as much as He allowed them to. We all know that Jesus chose 12 disciples for Himself and then another 70 disciples to be with Him and learn from Him (see Mark 6:13-14, Luke 10:1). However, while Jesus had other disciples, Peter, James, and John stood out the most. But why? What made them so special? Why does the Bible specifically highlight Peter, James, and

John? After all, they weren't better or more gifted than the other disciples. Was it Jesus' choice to be close to them, or was it the personal choice of Peter, James, and John to be close to Jesus?

Let's dig deeper. When Jesus retreated into deep prayer and was in agony at the Garden of Gethsemane, Peter, James, and John were close by. The Bible does not mention Judas, Matthew, or the other disciples there. Jesus asked the disciples, "Who do you say I am?" Peter was the first to confess Jesus as Lord. During the Last Supper, Jesus spent time with His disciples, and John leaned on His chest and asked Him questions. Jesus didn't have favorites. Jesus never said, "Hey, Peter is pretty cool, huh? I think I'll take him with Me everywhere. John is a pretty fun person, so I'll take him, too." That is not how the Kingdom of God operates. Jesus wouldn't have taken these three disciples with Him if He hadn't seen their attitude towards Him and their devotion to the Lord. Let's examine it more in the Scripture.

On the evening of His arrest, before the crucifixion, a wave of fear swept over all the disciples, and they all scattered. Who remained with Him and ventured to enter the high priest's courtyard? Peter did. Who remained faithful at the cross? It was John. When Jesus was resurrected, who ran to His tomb? Peter and John did. I don't see any of the other disciples running there. Why? Where was Phillip? What about Matthew? Andrew wasn't there either? Huh. Who jumped out of the boat and swam to the shore with a heart ablaze, ready to meet Jesus? Peter did. All the others chose the safety of the boat. Their demeanor speaks of their dedication and attitude towards Jesus Himself.

Sometimes, people ask me ,"Why did you appoint these people to be pastors? Why did you choose these people for your team? Is it because they're your friends? Are you showing favoritism?" Not at all. The ministers who become part of my team aren't there because I like them more or know them personally. They're there because of their dedication to God

Himself. Their dedication is not to me, a ministry, but to God Himself. Promotion comes from God.

God didn't play favorites when He invited Peter, James, and John to come up higher and experience a greater revelation of Himself through Jesus. More than the other disciples, their devotion to Jesus was evident in every sphere of their lives.

Notice that all the disciples were actively involved in ministry; they healed, cast out demons, and preached; however, ministry successes and miracles don't determine how close you are to Jesus. So many times, I've been told, "God loves you more. That's why you're close to Him." Absolutely not! Neither God, your ministry, nor your calling determine how close you are to Him. It's entirely based on your decision and dedication to God Himself. I, alone, have the power to decide how close I want to be to God by dedicating myself wholeheartedly to Him and setting aside distractions so that I can be with the Lord.

All of us, as disciples, are called to be with Jesus and learn from Him so that we can be transformed into His likeness. However, the extent of our dedication, the depth of our learning, and the closeness we experience with Jesus doesn't depend on Him; it depends on us.

Value the Time You Have

Pause for a moment and think about your life. What hinders you from being close to God? How much time do you spend with Him in your secret place? Most people spend 30 minutes, some one hour, or even 2 hours with Him, but many don't go any further. What prevents you from being with God more? What blocks you from hearing the voice of the Holy Spirit? I understand we all have responsibilities we can't ignore.

I'm not trying to push you to some extreme. I'm just asking, "Do you value the time you have?"

A young woman once wrote to me:

"Greetings, Pastor Andrey. What should I do? When I listened to your teaching about closeness with God, I was literally crushed inside. I want to dedicate myself to the Lord and spend time with Him, but I have five little children. I physically don't have any time to myself. I'm so busy. I try hard to set aside time to be with God, even a little bit. But then, every night, after putting my kids to sleep, cleaning the house, and preparing for the following day, I only have 15 minutes. I just lock myself in a room and weep because I only have 15 minutes to be with God. But I want to be close to Him, know Him and hear His voice."

As I was reading her message, I heard the voice of the Holy Spirit inside my heart, *Tell her she can't even imagine how precious these 15 minutes are to Me. I always wait for her there. Tell her to keep going and not to stop. This time is valuable in My eyes. I will expand her opportunities and lead her further.*

Some people have time and don't value it; others cry because they only have 15 minutes to spend alone with God. Yes, maybe it's only for 15 minutes, but still, this mother is building an altar of intimacy with God. Her sacrifice is a pleasing fragrance before the Lord. Jesus spoke highly of such sacrifices when talking about the widow and her two coins, "(She) has given more than all the rest…" Trust me, this doesn't just apply to finances only; it also applies to time. Time is a valuable resource that we should steward properly and dedicate to God. This widow gave everything she had. It's written:

> *Truly I say to you that this poor widow has put in more than all; for all these out of their abundance have put in*

offerings for God, but she out of her poverty put in all the livelihood that she had (Luke 21:3-4).

I want to encourage people in similar circumstances: God sees your sacrifice. Don't limit God and what He can do in your life with your 15 minutes when you consistently show up to the secret place. You will see the fruit. You are building an altar. Keep going. Keep doing it. You will reap the reward.

God has determined for each of us a time and place of our dwelling so we might seek the Lord and find Him (see Acts 17:26-27). Value the time you have. Determine your priorities and values. Then, steward your time and build an altar of intimacy with God.

Come Out of the Camp

One important thing to grasp and always remember is that the secret place is not for you to intercede or seek something, although God may lead you to intercession. The secret place isn't for you to prepare for a sermon, although God can give you a word that He wants you to communicate to a church. Therefore, you don't come to the secret place with the intention of getting something. You come to the secret place for Him, to earnestly come to know Him, and to be with Him, period. When I'm in the secret place, He comes in a way where my physical body begins to react and feel God. It's as if a celestial cloud fills that place and completely covers me. If you experience God's presence in your prayer time, try to linger; do not rush through those moments as if you've reached your goal. Don't leave as soon as you feel His presence. Linger a little longer and stay in that atmosphere. Remember, you are in the secret place not to feel His presence but for Him. Don't get me wrong, I relish experiencing God and feeling His blissful anointing, but that's not what I should be looking for. My goal is God Himself, His Person, and what He will say to me. That's why I urge you not to leave as soon as you experience His presence. Allow Him to teach you and lead you further in knowing Him.

While studying the Scriptures, I suddenly realized that those who were close to God didn't just practice the secret place. They also practiced solitude or retreating with God. What do I mean? They purposely set aside all their busyness and went away to intentionally spend time with Him, to get to know Him. Jesus had His secret place with the Father, but Jesus also made it a habit of retreating with God. Scripture tells us that He often withdrew to the wilderness, and there were instances where He spent 40 days entirely alone with the Father.

One day, I was faced with a question that made me tremble, "Andrey, what's disrupting God from being close to you?" I started examining my life. What if God wants to speak with me, but I'm not available, my busyness, ministry, or other things don't let Him? What things in my life keep me from a close relationship with Him? After all, He wants me to be wholly devoted to Him, not to the ministry or the church. That way, He can minister through me. *Am I too busy with ministry to the point where I can't just stop and be with God?* These thoughts filled me with the fear of God, and I answered: "God, I'm all yours. I'm ready to pay the price and adjust my schedule. I will find time and opportunities so that nothing will stand between You and me. I want to go further."

When I was struck with God's electric power in my secret room, God called me to go further and expand that alone time with Him. I understood that I needed to take practical steps and just go for it, not wait. After all, He was waiting for me. I sensed I needed to retreat to be with God in the mountains. Why? Well, I cherish my family dearly, but it was evident I couldn't do it at home considering all the distractions.

I needed to leave the city, detach from what's ordinary, and ascend the mountain to be with Him.

Some may argue that there is no need to get away because you can spend time with God anywhere, including your house. Of course you can. However, there is a reason why Jesus went away to the desert places. There is a reason why King David went to the Mount of Olives and worshiped God there. There is a reason why Moses put the Tent of Meeting outside the camp and went there often to pray and fellowship with God. And there is a reason why all those who sought God started coming there, too. The hunger to be with God drew them there. This hunger for God brought them out of the camp while the rest of the people were busy with the hustle and bustle of life.

Interestingly, not all people went to the tent to worship, only those who sought the Lord. Others chose to stay and pray in the camp. They were content with business as usual. They just prayed to God in their circumstances. They didn't feel the need to present themselves to the Lord physically.

If you still think that retreating with God is a wild idea, then let me assure you that many places in Scripture reinforce this practice. Some of you even cite these Scriptures without realizing how to exercise them. Psalm 46 says:

Be still, and know that I am God (Psalm 46:10).

To know the Lord, we have to stop and be still before Him.

My First Time in the Mountains with God

Filled with an overwhelming desire to deepen my connection with God, I decided to go to the mountains and extend my 30 minutes to a three-day retreat with God. I found a modest yet cozy hotel room in the mountains, grabbed my guitar and Bible, and set off in anticipation of an encounter with God. Little did I know that I would "die" there. Yes, you read that right. I was dying to myself. See, I am a people person; I thrive in the company of others. I like being around people, doing ministry, gathering our team, organizing projects, and so on. I like movement. And suddenly, I were there alone for three days.

I didn't fully understand what I was supposed to do for three days or what a retreat with God was even supposed to look like. I walked into my hotel room and closed the door. And so there I was, alone with God. What do I even do? Well, I started with prayer. One hour went by. What's next? I read my Bible. Another hour went by. What's next? I guess I'll worship. Another hour went by. At this point, I was exhausted. I put my guitar to the side, sat on the couch, and thought, "What on earth! Only three hours passed, and I'm supposed to be here for three days. What am I going to do?" I prayed some more. Another thirty minutes went by. I read. Okay, then what's next?

I was clueless. This sudden halt in activity began to stress me out more than I thought it would. The silence became a source of frustration, forcing me to see my true self. I began to see my attachment to the visible world in this stillness. In this pause, this moment of reflection, I discovered my inner condition. Everything rose to the surface: my feelings, emotions, desires, plans, tiredness, and worries. They were never at rest. It seemed like everything was weighing on me and talking to me except for God.

However, I wasn't going to give up that easily. I told myself that I must press in. If a job is once begun, never leave until it's done. With this mindset, I revisited the New Testament and delved into the teaching. I was seriously determined to uncover a great revelation there. But the more I read, I couldn't help but notice all the references to food. Jesus multiplied bread and fish, a great story, and I like fish. The disciples began picking the heads of grain and eating. These chapters only intensified my hunger, taking my attention away from God and directing it toward my growling stomach. My fatigue screamed. It turns out I didn't know myself. I didn't realize that my body, feelings, and emotions have such an influence on my life that I could not calm them down to hear God. Once again, everything except for God seemed to be speaking to me.

I barely made it to evening. You know what I did next? I went to sleep as soon as it got dark. Usually, I go to bed late, but that day, I was at a loss for what to do, so I decided to go to sleep around 9-10 p.m.

I woke up early and thought, "No, Andrey, sleep more. You never wake up this early." So, I listened to my instincts and dozed off again till 10:00 a.m. I got my fill of sleep. I felt good for a second, and then my conscience started condemning me, "Did you come here to sleep?" Little did I know that God had a purpose in allowing me to rest. Our physical bodies need to rest to be at peace. When you're well-rested, your mind is sharper, making it easier to pray and read the Bible. Your body has to find rest before your soul can. So, to hear God, it is essential that your physical body and soul are in harmony.

To help myself refocus, I brewed a fresh cup of coffee, turned on some worship, and walked around the room, praying and admiring the mountains outside my window. However, I didn't hear God speak to me. To be honest, I couldn't help but feel disappointed that I didn't hear God during this whole time. My mind was distracted by the ticking clock, the stunning view, the room's layout, and my upcoming projects and plans.

During those three days, I was experiencing these "withdrawal" symptoms as all the movement and vanity in my life suddenly came to a halt. Have you ever come to your place of prayer, but your thoughts are everywhere else? Or perhaps you went to church to hear God's Word, but you're thinking about your business. You set aside some time to be with God, but you're thinking about your family, ministry, circumstances, worries, or other random things. Everything is a distraction that pulls you away.

Anyway, I concluded that I have to plan out every hour. I devoted an hour to prayer, an hour to read, an hour to worship, and then took a break for an hour. And then again, an hour of each: Prayer, reading, worship, and rest. I made an hourly schedule. When evening rolled around on the second day, I had many thoughts piercing my mind, "Run! Get out of there and stop torturing yourself. Why are you wasting your time doing this? You have no encounters here. This kind of practice doesn't fit your personality..." Those thoughts were weighing on me, but I chose to push through and stay committed instead of relying on feelings. Then, I went to sleep early again.

Much like the previous two days, not much happened on day three. But in the evening, right before leaving, I suddenly sensed clarity and freedom enveloping my mind, something I had never experienced. This lightness was in my body, soul, and my thoughts. Reading the Bible became effortless, and God's Word seemed to flow into me. I was captivated, eagerly reading chapter after chapter.

I returned home happy. I did it. For three days, I was with God. Except nothing happened. Nothing supernatural, at least. I didn't see any angels or their wings. And sure, I read the Word and was filled, but that's it. I came home, and you know what I noticed? I was different. I looked around and thought, "Everything's so fast. What's everyone rushing for? Why's everyone so anxious?" I felt different. I felt a sense of tranquility and peace that can only be described as divine. I even noticed that my reactions were different. It was the beginning of a remarkable journey.

However, all I remembered after that first trip was how hard of an experience it was. I didn't understand why God called me into solitude with Him or what He was trying to accomplish in me. Trust me, I didn't want to go again and be there alone for three days. It was too difficult. It cost me too much. Nevertheless, I heard His voice within me, "Continue on this path. Don't stop. I'm separating you for Myself."

"Lord, but nothing happened on that retreat…"

Seven Days of Silence

After the Israelites crossed the Red Sea, God called Moses to ascend to the mountain (see Exodus 24:12). When he went up, God didn't talk to him for six days; He only spoke on the seventh day. Have you ever wondered why?

Imagine Moses on the mountain waiting for God. Most likely, he didn't understand why nothing was happening, why he was sitting there, why he was waiting, and most importantly, why God was silent. I'm confident that God was ready to speak to Moses on the first day, but in Moses's state, he couldn't hear God correctly and receive what God wanted to tell him. *What do I mean?* Think about it: Moses led the children of Israel out of Egypt. Over a million people. It was an enormous victory and an enormous responsibility for Moses. Moses' ministry was one of massive proportions. He led a nation with all its belongings, problems, arguments, circumstances, choices, and uncertainties. Moses had to take care of all of this. His mind was under much pressure from his responsibilities and ministry to people. And God saw that ministry took up so much of his mental capacity that he couldn't hear God or receive His commandments and plans properly in the camp. Yes, in all this, Moses needed God to fulfill His ministry and calling, but God also needed Moses to further reveal His plan and will. For this reason, God separated Moses from all the busyness and called him up to the mountain. Mount Sinai blazed and thundered—God consecrated that place for Himself.

And so, as Moses was on the mountain, waiting on God, God was waiting on Moses. What do I mean by "waiting"? Well, have you ever talked to somebody who feels anxious? You meet up, but the other person just talks and talks. You try to say something, but it's as if they can't hear you. This person doesn't just need to stop talking; they must calm down to listen to you properly. Jesus said, "Those who have ears, let them hear." This means you can have ears but can't hear or comprehend what you hear. If you stopped talking but didn't stop everything going on inside of you, you won't be able to hear properly.

Therefore, it was not Moses who waited for God to speak for seven days; it was God Who waited for Moses to calm down. God didn't want to talk with Moses' emotions, tiredness, feelings, or opinions. God was waiting for this to calm down and for Moses to enter into rest so He could speak with Moses himself. Seven days went by. I believe that by then, Moses rested and was no longer thinking about people, needs, ministry, or what was happening in his life. All of that faded into the background. Do you know what happened after he calmed down? He took this position before God:

> *I will stand my watch and set myself on the rampart, and watch to see what He will say to me, and what I will answer when I am corrected (Habakkuk 2:1).*

God waited until Moses was ready to receive. God waited because what He planned to give Moses wasn't just for Moses and his ministry but His plan for many generations.

I Went There Again

The following month, I left again for three days. At the time, I didn't understand that God was teaching me to enter His rest. This time, I tried a different approach to spending time with God. I brought along sermon recordings, worship recordings, my guitar, and the Bible, among other things. I tried fasting. I read, prayed, sat silently, and alternated between these practices. I was learning to calm my feelings and emotions and immerse myself in His peace. I was learning to experience His presence and direct my undivided attention toward God.

Despite my hectic schedule and considerable financial hardships, I continued to spend time alone with God every month for three days. Honestly, there were many instances where I didn't experience anything supernatural; however, upon returning home, I noticed a difference in my inner condition. Soon, I started to learn to live from this state of rest and operate in the visible world from God's presence. It was a gradual process. After some time, I learned to focus on God instead of paying attention to the clock, window, and mountains while looking at them. I could be with people but not focus on them anymore. My attention was on Him and what He would say to me. I could sit in a busy café or the serenity of nature, and be so engrossed in His Word that the visible world ceased to distract me. On those retreats, I learned to give all my attention to Him, listen to His voice, and gaze upon His glory.

Holy Spirit, Teach me!

Once again, I went on another retreat with God in the mountains, praying the whole way there and thinking, "What am I doing wrong? Why is there no breakthrough?" I've already tried all the methods I knew of. Something was missing. Honestly, I liked my condition when I got back home. I wouldn't say I liked going there because I was always dying to myself. There, everything in me suffered. Sometimes, I felt like I was just wasting my time and money for three days. I was driving and thinking about this. And in my head, one thought was going round and round: "…the Holy Spirit, whom the Father will send in My name, He will teach you all things, and bring to your remembrance all things that I said to you…" (John 14:26).

I checked in, entered the hotel room, and sat on the couch. I realized that I couldn't enjoy these days if I didn't allow God to show me how He sees these retreats in the first place. I took the Bible in my hands, knelt before God, and said:

"Holy Spirit, teach me. I'll be honest, and please forgive me for saying this, but I'm tired of all this. It's so hard to do these retreats. I am still trying to figure out what to do next. I can't just keep cycling between prayer and reading. Please show me Your format and how You see this time."

And as if a rushing wind came over me, I heard Him say:

"I was waiting for that. This whole time, I was waiting for you to invite Me to teach you about this time with Me. I was waiting for you to try all your methods and schedules and realize that they won't work. Everything you practiced were things that others taught you to do. You took someone else's model without even realizing."

I had some fantastic conversations with God on that retreat.

Who Told You That?

Next, the Holy Spirit started asking me questions:

Who told you this, Andrey?

Who told you that time alone with God should look like this?

Who told you that church services are only supposed to be a certain way?

Who told you that worship to God should only be a certain way?

Who said that only certain songs and instruments have a place in the church?

Who told you that church is supposed to be structured and function this way?

What if you were to live on a deserted island and never met any Christians? Then suddenly, a Bible ended up in your hands, and you received Jesus. What would your Christianity look like?

I contemplated the methods, ministry models, church structure, worship formats, and all the practices that shaped me. I questioned the essence of my actions: Why do we do things the way we do? What would our Christianity look like if nobody taught us and we would rely only on God through His Word, devoid of people's experiences or opinions? What would be the schedule of church services? What would the church look like? What kind of format would we create if we didn't have models, the experiences of the generations before us, and the templates that are pushed on us nowadays as if they were the truth?

I said:

"God, I give up. I don't know where I got these methods, templates, or stereotypes. Teach me. Uproot everything that you did not plant in me. Show me Your way."

God said:

"Are you ready? Are you ready for Me to start teaching you?"

And here, my heart started racing. I heard not only the voice of the Lord but the intonation and power of His voice. I understood that behind the question, "Are you ready?" was a price to pay.

"You want Me to teach you? Do you know what this will cost you? If you want to be My disciple, you would have to lose your soul. If you want to be My disciple, you have to pick up your cross and follow Me. Are you ready to die to self?"

"But God, I thought I already did. What do You mean? What do You mean to take up your cross?"

He answered:

"The cross symbolizes My will. You will have to die to yourself daily to live in the will of the Father. Are you ready? Are you ready for Me to lead you there?"

At that moment, I was confident of one thing: I can't stop now. I want to go further in God. There is only one way to get there. God brought me to that moment. First, He waited for me to try everything, all my methods and approaches, all my knowledge formed by opinions and experiences of other people, and then turn to Him so that He could take every veil off me. After I came to this realization and calmed down all my feelings, emotions, and desires, He granted me this choice. He got to my will and my right to make a choice. At that moment, I surrendered my right to choose so He could fulfill His will through me.

"Yes, Lord. I want this. I am all Yours. Take me further. I am all Yours."

God replied:

"Then, I will not make a Christian out of you; I will make a son out of you so you will fulfill My purpose on this earth."

Let me explain: God didn't send His Spirit to make us Christians. The believers in Antioch started being called "Christians" in the first place (see Acts 11:26). I'm not against the name "Christians," but the Lord didn't give us that name. It came from people, so it would be easier for them to categorize people's religious affiliations. God's desire from the beginning was to adopt you and me and make you His son or daughter, not just a Christian.

"Alright, God. Make me a son. How will You do this?"

"According to My image and likeness. This is why you need to know the Word. You will learn the original design and plan so you don't copy someone else's blueprint."

"Sounds good. Are we starting in Genesis?"

He says:

"No, start with John chapter 1."

"Why John? You started everything in Genesis."

"Yes, I did this once, so I had to do away with the former to establish the latter. Open the first chapter of John and dive into the words of Jesus:

> *In the beginning was the Word, and the Word was with God, and the Word was God. He was in the beginning with God. All things were made through Him, and without Him nothing was made that was made. In Him was life, and the life was the light of men. And the light shines in the darkness, and the darkness did not comprehend it (John 1:1-5).*

And from that day forth, my retreats with God had changed. I began to see time with God differently. I understood that I must connect more with the Word of God, so I started focusing more on the Scripture. The Word is not the letter, but the Spirit which gives life. Through the Word, the Holy Spirit teaches me His language so that I would think as He does, and He can lead me further.

Sometimes, people ask me, "How much time do you give to prayer, and how much do you give to the Word when you spend time with God in the mountains?" The bond I share with God is inseparable from His Word. For me, this is one and the same. The Holy Spirit is one with the Word, speaking through the Word and making the Word alive within you. Through this connection, Jesus' presence becomes tangible in our lives. That's why I can't separate prayer from the Word.

The Words of Jesus

I want to draw your attention to what happened on the Mount of Transfiguration:

> *Now after six days Jesus took Peter, James, and John his brother, led them up on a high mountain by themselves; and He was transfigured before them. His face shone like the sun, and His clothes became as white as the light. And behold, Moses and Elijah appeared to them, talking with Him. Then Peter answered and said to Jesus, "Lord, it is good for us to be here; if You wish, let us make here three tabernacles: one for You, one for Moses, and one for Elijah."*
>
> *While he was still speaking, behold, a bright cloud overshadowed them; and suddenly a voice came out of the*

cloud, saying, "This is My beloved Son, in whom I am well pleased. Hear Him!" And when the disciples heard it, they fell on their faces and were greatly afraid. But Jesus came and touched them and said, "Arise, and do not be afraid." When they had lifted up their eyes, they saw no one but Jesus only (Matthew 17:1-8).

And so, Peter, James, and John went up on a high mountain with Jesus to pray. Most likely, they were climbing up for a few days. Notice again that the other disciples didn't go up the mountain; they stayed below with everyone else. I'm sure they had things to do, but these three went with Jesus. It's also written that Peter, James, and John fell asleep up there (see Luke 9:34-36), and when they woke up, they saw Jesus in His glory, and with Him were Moses and Elijah. This prophetic encounter held profound significance. Prophetically speaking, Moses represents the law, Elijah represents the prophets, and Jesus, the living Word of God made flesh (see John 1:16-18). Moses (the Law) was our guardian until Christ came; Elijah (the prophetic voice) represented all the prophets until John the Baptist. And from the days of John the Baptist, the Kingdom of God is preached.

Here's what's fascinating: When Peter sees Jesus, Moses, and Elijah, he puts all three of them on the same level, blurting out, "Let us build three tabernacles: one for You, one for Moses, and one for Elijah." A cloud descended over them as he spoke, and Moses and Elijah were taken from their sight. Only Jesus remained, and the voice of God roared from the cloud, *"This is My beloved Son. Listen to Him!"* (Luke 9:36). That was a divine moment that carried significant truth. All Scripture is inspired by God. I'm not against Moses (The Law), and I'm not against Elijah (Prophetic), but the Father Himself declared, "From now on, listen to Him!" Here is where the Holy Spirit led me to—the words of Jesus.

Today, many people read their Bible and spend more time in the Old Testament or the epistles than in Matthew, Mark, Luke, and John. By no means do I intend to belittle the rest of the Bible. However, I need you to understand that the epistles and books of the Bible were penned by the apostle Paul, apostle Peter, apostle John, Moses, and Elijah, who were divinely inspired through their intimate relationships with God. Undoubtedly, each of them had a strong bond with God. Nevertheless, it is crucial that we do not elevate these writings above the words of Jesus Himself.

The four Gospels perfectly show what the relationship between the Father and the Son looks like. The Holy Spirit prompted me to dwell in the four Gospels more than all the other books in the Bible so that I could see the Law of Moses, the prophets, the Old Testament, and even the book of Revelation through the words of Jesus. Friend, begin to study the words of Jesus and learn to understand all Scripture through His very words because He is the Way, the Truth, and the Life.

Yes, read the Old Testament, but dwell in the words of Jesus. Read Acts and the Epistles, but live in the words of Jesus. Study Revelation and the books of the prophets, but abide in the words of Jesus so that you can interpret all other Scriptures through the words of Jesus and not the other way around. Don't mix the Old and New Testament. Don't let Moses, Elijah, or anyone else overshadow Jesus for you. After all, Jesus revealed the Father to us.

> *If you abide in My word, you are My disciples indeed. And you shall know the truth, and the truth shall make you free (John 8:31-32).*

That day marked the beginning of a new era for my retreats with God. I removed all formats, assumptions, and agendas and began connecting with and diving into God's Word. Do you know what I noticed? Three days wasn't enough anymore! I needed more time. Why? I encountered the living Word that breathed new life into my soul. When I go to the mountains, my one desire is for the Word to speak to me and become flesh within me.

A Challenge

Many years have passed, and I have seen the colossal results of my retreats with God. Consistently, for over 20 years, I have engaged in these spiritual retreats, which gives me the boldness to teach about it. I challenge you, especially if you're a minister, to begin to retreat with God every month and learn to present yourself to Him. Start practicing what Jesus practiced. And remember that He practiced both the secret place and retreats with the Lord. Accept this challenge from me. You will see incredible fruit in your life and your walk with God.

How to start:

1. **Make a decision.** Don't wait for inspiration. Make the decision right now, choose a day, and mark your calendar. You might not feel anything at first, but don't stop. Keep going.

2. **Begin to practice.** Start doing it, and in the process, you will figure out what place works best for you and the time, rhythm, and how your time with God will look.

3. **Be Consistent.** Don't rush to conclusions, even if nothing is happening or you haven't received any revelations yet. Keep going despite how you might feel. Consistency is an essential element in your spiritual growth. That's how I see discipleship: It is consistent and purposeful. Consistency requires discipline. Keep going. You will surely start to see changes and transform into His image from

glory to glory, and the fruit of your relationship with God will become apparent.

4. **Make it your mission** to give yourself entirely to God and be devoted to Him till your last breath. Remember, God is the essence of our existence, our breath. You cannot live on one breath of air for the rest of your life. You need a constant supply of fresh air. Similarly, it's impossible to live off yesterday's intimacy with God. We live, breathe, and find our purpose in Him.

5. **Practice this retreat for the sake of the Lord Himself.** Never go on a retreat with God for something other than Him. Don't do this for ministry's sake, for a new sermon, for a problem you're dealing with, or because you're about to make an important decision. Don't allow ministry for God to replace intimacy with Him. Don't let ministry become your lord. Let God be your Lord, and let ministry be the overflow of that. In other words, you allow God to flow through you and do His work. You are becoming His vessel on earth.

Don't be afraid to let God take you further. Remember this: how close you are with God is your choice.

Chapter 7

We Celebrate The Lord!

*You shall worship the LORD your God,
and Him only you shall serve.*

Matthew 4:10

I am so grateful for the Holy Spirit, who is on this earth to lead us into sonship, the knowledge of God, and ultimate victory. Teaching about the Holy Spirit and cultivating a close relationship with Him brings me great joy. However, in this chapter, the Holy Spirit is prompting me to pause and talk about finances. You might ask, "Why money again? What does money have to do with intimacy with the Holy Spirit?" The truth is many of God's people lack understanding in this area, and as a result, they struggle. It's not about money; it's about being under His lordship in the realm of finances.

Unfortunately, I hear statements like these quite a bit:

"I wish I could go on a retreat with God for a few days, but I don't have enough money."

"I wish I could go on a mission trip, but I cannot afford it right now."

"I wish I could attend Bible college, but I don't have enough money."

"I wish I could do ministry full-time, but I don't have money; I have to provide for my family."

A person feels the call of God and wants to devote themselves to the Lord. They manage to work two jobs and serve in the local church. Yet, they don't have enough money to do more. They feel stuck. Does this sound familiar?

The devil has created this distorted image of God in our imaginations, making Him look like a Master who sent workers to His field without provision or like Pharaoh, who did not provide straw for the Israelites to make bricks and made them gather straw for themselves. Where does that image of God come from? Look what David says in Psalm 23:1: "The Lord is my Shepherd, I shall not want." We must learn to see the Father's heart rightly regarding our needs and understand what His lordship in our finances looks like.

God once told me, "If something doesn't work out in your life, it's because there's something you don't know." That is why God gave us His Holy Spirit to guide us in all truth. We must get to know Him and learn how to bring every area of our life under His lordship. Walking in the Holy Spirit leads to victory; there is only the total triumph of Jesus. Although, before the Holy Spirit does something great through you, He will first do a great work in you.

I remember a time in my life when I had a decent job that provided for all my family's needs. I was also able to pray a lot while I worked and had time to serve at my church afterward. Everything was going great. However, there came a moment when I heard the Lord tell me to go into full-time ministry. I got scared. How was I supposed to leave my job? The timing wasn't very convenient; I could feel my faith being challenged. I realized God was calling me to step out of the boat and walk on water. I remember saying to God, "I want to, but I need money to provide for my family. I have a wife and a toddler." The Holy Spirit responded: "Consecrate yourself to Me to do full-time ministry. I will give you opportunities to make extra money. I will lead you and will provide for you."

My wife and I talked it over, and in mutual agreement, we decided that I would quit my job and be sensitive to the Holy Spirit's leadership. Please note this decision was not based on emotions or feelings. I mention this because some say, "I don't want to work—I want to serve God full-time." No, I wasn't being lazy, nor was I led by feelings. When I heard the command from the Lord, I had to obey His voice despite my feelings.

So, I left my job and entirely devoted myself to God and church ministry. Some time passed, and we began to experience financial difficulties. We didn't have money to cover the basic needs for our little daughter. I have never neglected physical labor; in fact, I could have devoted my time and started my own business to provide for the family, and I'm sure I would've succeeded. But then again, God did say, "Give yourself entirely to Me. I will give you opportunities to make extra money and lead you. I will provide for you." So, I had a word from God, but no money left. I remember how I locked myself in the room and began praying in the Spirit. It troubled me that I could not provide for my family's needs as a man and a father. I didn't ask God for money. I struggled to understand why God promised one thing, but in reality, things looked different. So, I resorted to just praying in tongues.

It was a breaking point for me. I had to make a decision. I remember saying to myself, "Andrey, you are not going back to work two jobs and overwork yourself trying to make time to do God's work. You are done living paycheck to paycheck. Your time being under the world's system for the dollar to dictate how much time you give to God and ministry is over. You will not worship finances. You will worship the Lord your God and serve Him only." I was bold in my prayer.

A Scripture popped into my mind. Once, God told Joshua, "I have given you the land from the wilderness to the river Euphrates, and from Jordan to the Great Sea. The land is yours. Therefore, go and take it into your possession" (see Joshua 1:2-4). In other words, God declared, "Joshua, the land is yours. You must now conquer in the physical world what I have given you in the spiritual." Well, I also received a word from God and knew that in the spiritual realm, it was already finished. God made me a promise—I am already blessed. The provision was there for me. I just had trouble accessing that blessing. I didn't know how to unlock and open the door to allow the manifestation of what had already been accomplished in the spiritual realm to materialize *in the physical world*.

I was pacing back and forth, praying in tongues out loud with this revelation in mind. All of a sudden, a surge of boldness washed over me. I took the last dollar bill I had out of my pocket, looked at it, and holy jealousy rose within me. I began to speak to the dollar bill: *In Jesus' name, I will not worship you. I will not serve your financial system. You will serve me! We will worship God and serve Him alone.* Speaking to the dollar bill, I spoke to the entire financial system of this world. I pointed my finger at it and said: *You will serve God's purposes! Do you understand me, dollar? You will serve God's plans!* I spoke with such boldness and authority that I almost tore it in half. Well, I "put it in its place". And at that very moment, my phone rang.

"Here is your answer," I heard the voice of the Holy Spirit.

I usually don't have my phone on when I go to pray, but this time it was both on and in my pocket. I checked the caller ID, and it was my cousin. I thought, "How could the answer come from my cousin?"

"This is your answer," I heard the Holy Spirit say again.

I picked up the phone and said:

"Hey Igor."

And the first thing he said was:

"Bro, do you want to make some extra cash?"

"I do. How much do you pay? And what kind of job do I need to do?"

"There's work for 2 hours at most, and I'll pay you $100."

"Deal. I'm on my way."

I was driving and thanking God, "This is incredible. We can buy everything we need for the baby and even have money left over to buy groceries."

David proclaims the following about the lordship of God: *"He leads me in the paths of righteousness for His name's sake"* (Psalm 23:3). God leads you. Note that He never forces you—He guides you. That means He gives you ideas and insights on what you should do to lead you into His provision. You need to understand this concept about His lordship. Some people only pray that God will bless them financially but don't do anything. They need to realize that money won't just miraculously fall in their lap from heaven. In the lordship of God, blessings come from His voice and obedience to Him.

So, I arrived at my cousin's job site. He had a business in interior home renovations. We started working, and I shared about what God was doing. For two hours straight, we talked about His reality and power. Sometimes, I get so captivated by the reality of God that I don't always notice that all I talk about is Him, the things He does, His miracles and wonders, and what He's revealing to me. We didn't talk about my financial circumstances at all; we only discussed ways of God and His miracles. Two hours flew by like 20 minutes.

When the work was done, I washed my hands and went outside. My cousin was writing me a check on the hood of his car. He paused, looked at me nervously, and said:

"Here's your check. Thank you. You can leave now."

I looked at it. The check was for $500.

"Bro?!"

"You can leave. There isn't much profit in having you work for me."

"Why?"

"For two hours straight as we were working, the Holy Spirit kept telling me: "It's $500, not $100. Give him $500. It's $500, not $100..." Just take your money and go. You are not a profitable employee."

I have many more testimonies of God's financial provision. He is forever faithful! When you allow the Lord to be your Shepherd, you won't experience lack. He will lead your steps, inspire you with ideas, and give you both opportunities and favor, touching the hearts of others and blessing both you and them. Let me highlight something—you won't be able to live under God's full provision if you don't grasp the concept of His lordship in finances.

Please understand that only some are called to be in full-time ministry. However, everyone is called to use their God-given gifts to fulfill His purpose and will. Trust me, you need resources and provision to fulfill your calling just like I do.

It's not about finances only. You might not have financial difficulties, but you have other areas where you experience defeat or serious challenges. God wants to bring freedom to every area of your life because He wants to become the Lord of your **whole life**.

I know for a fact that God wants to do immeasurably more in your life than you can think or imagine. I know for a fact that God wants to bless you to the point that you have no sorrows in your life so you can fulfill His will. I know for a fact that His will for you is good, pleasing, and perfect. I know for a fact that Jesus came to give you life and life more abundantly. MORE ABUNDANTLY! (see John 10:10). Let's be honest—your children not serving the Lord is not "life more abundantly."

Similarly, when you get sick, when curses operate in your life, or when you experience financial difficulties, such things are not "life more abundantly." Such things clearly show that you need deliverance, freedom, and a more profound revelation of the truth in those areas. But remember, complete deliverance is a process. The devil won't give up easily. He will do whatever it takes to keep you bound.

When Moses led the Israelites out of Egypt, Pharaoh was stubborn and didn't want to let them go. He clung to every area, word, and anything within his grasp to obstruct the fulfillment of God's plan. The book of Exodus prophetically foreshadows our time. Egypt represents the system of this world, Pharaoh represents the devil, and the Israelites leaving Egypt represents our liberation from the system of this world.

Moses Voiced the Will of God

The book of Exodus describes how the Israelites were enslaved by the Egyptians, who built their kingdom and infrastructure at the expense of the Israelites' heavy labor. Ancient Egypt, a civilization of significant influence and grandeur, achieved remarkable advancements in culture, science, architecture, and technology. Having been raised in Pharaoh's palace, Moses was taught all their knowledge and was familiar with their government system. Moses was well aware that Pharaoh was considered and held the status of an exalted, divine ruler, exerting total control over Egyptians' lives. Consequently, his people revered him deeply.

The Scriptures record Moses and Aaron coming to Pharaoh with the word of the Lord:

Let My people go, that they may hold a feast to Me in the wilderness (Exodus 5:1).

Pharaoh didn't agree and would never let Israel go if it weren't for the horrific, deadly plagues taking place. The situation worsened, and Pharaoh's officials pleaded with him:

Pharaoh's officials said to him, "How long will this man be a snare to us? Let the people go so that they may worship the Lord their God. Do you not yet realize that Egypt is ruined?" Then Moses and Aaron were brought back to Pharaoh. "Go, worship the Lord your God, he said. But tell me who will be going" (Exodus 10:7-8 NIV).

Note that God sent Moses to deliver the people. To answer the Pharaoh's question: "Who will go with you?", Moses replied:

> *"We will go with our young and our old; with our sons and our daughters, with our flocks and our herds we will go, for we must hold a feast to the Lord" (Exodus 10:9).*

In other words, Moses said, "We must celebrate and have a feast to the Lord! All of us will come out of the system of this world, and we will take all our resources, too."

> *Then he said to them, "The Lord had better be with you when I let you and your little ones go! Beware, for evil is ahead of you. Not so! Go now, you who are men, and serve the LORD, for that is what you desired. And they were driven out of Pharaoh's presence" (Exodus 10:10-11).*

I want you to see the devil's strategy, "I am willing to let you go. But why do you need your children with you? Let them stay here. They will distract you from serving the Lord. Leave them here. They are too young to serve God. They don't understand anything yet. Only the men should go and serve God."

This has become a tragedy for many generations: many men fell for this trick and began to serve God alone, leaving their families behind. They became so busy serving God and giving all their energy and attention to building a ministry for Him that they forgot about their children. They believed the children weren't that important. Sadly, we see this taking place throughout many generations, and it's still happening in ours. Men preach to one another. They fight over the Bible verses, trying to prove their theology to everybody. They preserve their religion. They fight for traditions, forms of serving, titles, positions, and a place behind the pulpit. Meanwhile, the devil is infiltrating their children's minds through the internet, ungodly celebrities, and other people's influence and actions. Pharaoh agreed, "Surly men can go. Serve God. Fight for positions. Leave the children behind." While men battle for positions and traditions, their children get drunk and high, get addicted to pornography, games, and gambling, and as a result, they become full of fear, depression, and all kinds of perversion.

I want to make it clear that I am not throwing stones of condemnation at anyone. I want to address these issues to all believers. God told us through Moses to journey together. That is His will: The elderly and the youth, those in between, the sons and the daughters, our resources. And not a hoof should be left behind for the devil. All means all.

Unfortunately, the older generation often opposes and criticizes the youth, not giving them opportunities to rise and begin to minister and serve God. Let's learn to see further beyond ourselves and our time. Remember, God's thoughts are through all generations (see Psalm 33:11). Always encourage the next generation and invest time and resources into them. Men, we need to host conferences for kids, teens, and youth. We must teach them how to have intimacy with God and build personal relationships with the Holy Spirit. They're God's children, just as we are, and they are the ones who will carry God's faith forward beyond what we can. They will pass it on to the next generation. Let me emphasize: We should pass on **God's faith** to the next generations, not our **traditions**.

Psalm 78 encourages us:

> *We will not hide them from their children, telling to the generation to come the praises of the LORD, and His strength and His wonderful works that He has done (Psalm 78:4).*

This is what we need to pass on to our children—God's power, His miracles, and wonders and tell them about the works of God. Let the forms of service, methods, and approaches to ministry change. Our children should not adopt our traditions, religion, and service formats but must encounter God's reality, love, and power. They all need to experience the

We Celebrate The Lord!

Holy Spirit. I urge you to forget your traditions and focus on revealing the living God to your children.

Let me also address the attitudes of some young people who believe the older generation is outdated and redundant. I want to remind you how God sees it. His will is for all to walk together, young and old, sons and daughters, with all our resources.

My dear friend, to fulfill God's will on earth, we must walk shoulder to shoulder. We shouldn't criticize other generations or push each other away, but walk together. As for me and my house, we will serve the Lord, the One God and Father of all, who is above all, and through all, and in you all (see Ephesians 4:6).

Give Us Sacrifices!

After God sent the next plague and the exodus of Israel was near, Pharaoh called Moses again:

> *Then Pharaoh called to Moses and said, "Go, serve the Lord; only let your flocks and your herds be kept back. Let your little ones also go with you" (Exodus 10:24).*

In other words, Pharaoh said, "Fine, I'll let you go with your children to serve God but leave the finances." Their flocks and herds represented their finances; they were enslaved, so they didn't have much silver or gold.

So, Pharaoh let them leave, but without provision. Let this serve as a prophetic lesson for us. Many believers have realized that their children need to serve God with them. They began to walk together and fulfill God's will, but a lack of resources stopped them and started to pull them back into slavery. I know some missionaries who devote themselves to

God with their children but are constantly burdened financially. It almost feels like God sent them but withheld provision from them. Yet, you won't find anywhere in the Bible that the apostle Paul faced financial constraints preventing him from planting a church. So, what is the reason behind this issue?

Let me expose a strategy the adversary uses against God's people. You go into ministry, and you use all your gifts and anointing to do the will of God; however, if the necessary finances are withheld from you, you will become dependent on wealthy people, who, through their donations, can easily manipulate you and tell you how to run your ministry, what you should teach and what not teach, what you should do and not do. Then, it's no longer the Lord who is your shepherd but your sponsors. I am not talking about financial partnership in ministry; Jesus had financial partners. I'm talking about when people use donations to manipulate ministers. Alternatively, you become a slave of the financial system of the world. You go to church on Sunday and worship God, but from Monday to Friday, honor the system and be enslaved to it, investing all your talents, skills, and energy to make money. And every time, after a week of work, you would be so tired that you would have little or no time and energy left to spend time with the Lord. If this is the case, you won't be able to fulfill God's will on this earth.

Even though many people have come out of spiritual slavery, they are still in bondage in the area of finances. That is why God is prompting me to speak about this issue. The last thing Pharaoh will try to hold back from you is provision, "Go, serve your God. I'll watch how much you can do."

> *But Moses said, "You must also **give us sacrifices** and burnt offerings, that we may sacrifice to the Lord our God. Our livestock also shall go with us; not a hoof shall be left behind. For we must take some of them to serve the Lord*

our God, and even we do not know with what we must serve the Lord until we arrive there" (Exodus 10:25-26).

The LORD Determines the Sacrifice

I like how Moses responded, "You must also give us sacrifices!" And then he explains it further, "We don't determine how much to sacrifice; the Lord does. That's why we're taking everything, and the Lord will determine the sacrifice." It's brilliant!

Let me reiterate: when your finances are under God, He is the One who determines the sacrifice. Moses exclaimed, "I don't know how much God will ask for. It doesn't depend on me. Therefore, I can't leave anything in Egypt. It all belongs to the Lord. He is the Lord of everything we are connected to. Therefore, we must give our sacrifices as He determines! Not a hoof shall be left behind!"

God Himself is interested in giving you all the resources so that He could determine the sacrifice—this is according to the Scriptures. If you are the one deciding how much to give or sacrifice to the Lord, then He's not the Lord of your finances. That's what people who are in total control of their finances do. However, when the Lord is your shepherd, He appoints the sacrifice, not you. I'm not saying that you must give God everything. **Don't sacrifice everything but sacrifice everything He asks you to.**

As a side note, I needed to touch on donations, offerings, and sacrifices to display what God's total lordship in finances is all about. If we don't teach people to sacrifice, we will be held accountable before God for holding back the sources of blessing needed for the last Great Harvest.

Everyone wants to be blessed, but not everyone understands the concepts and principles of God's Kingdom. The path to live a more abundant life is often hindered by the fear of giving to God sacrificially. Remember that the measure in which we give will ultimately be measured back to us.

Learn to be led by God in finances so that He can determine the sacrifice and bless you so that you will be rich in every good work. Here is the little secret: the ground where you sow your financial seed holds value and significance. Choose wisely and sow into fertile soil that nurtures the preaching of the gospel. That fertile soil will bring forth an abundant harvest in your life.

Convince Every Person

In the next chapter, God speaks to Moses, instructing him:

> *"Speak now in the hearing of the people* (**means convince every person**)*, and let every man ask from his neighbor and every woman from her neighbor, articles of silver and articles of gold." And the Lord gave the people favor in the sight of the Egyptians. Moreover, the man Moses was very great in the land of Egypt, in the sight of Pharaoh's servants, and in the sight of the people (Exodus 11:2-3).*

In other words, God says, "I want to restore everything that the devil has stolen from you over the years! I want to return it to you because your resources are connected with your calling and the Last Harvest." God gave the Israelites such favor that they didn't just leave Egypt with what they had; they plundered Egypt, taking all the gold and silver with them.

The Israelites were loaded with silver, all gold, and all necessary provisions. Because God says, "The silver is Mine, and the gold is Mine," some people probably thought that they just got really lucky. It wasn't an unexpected lottery win; it was God's provision for what was to come. It all had a purpose.

Unfortunately, some people hold money too close to their hearts. They have been given the ability to do business and make money, but they use it solely for personal enrichment. In God's eyes, such people are poor because they put their trust in their savings. They save up and rely on the amount of money they have in their account.

In God's eyes, everything is measured by how much we surrender and let Him be the Lord of our lives. Under His lordship, we have access to boundless blessings. But, that doesn't mean we will all have lots of savings in the bank. It means we will have no need for anything because the Lord is our Shepherd; it's a transformative shift that allows us to live without any lack or want.

God had a purpose for taking the silver and gold from Egypt. It was connected to serving Him, the Tabernacle, and the First Temple. When God commanded Israel to build the Tabernacle, and later the Temple, God said to the people, "Now bring the silver and gold for the Temple where My presence will dwell." The glory of the First Temple was so great that people from all over the earth went to admire it. And this was only the Old Testament, a foreshadowing of the New Covenant.

The Glory of the Latter House

I want to share a prophetic understanding of what God is restoring in the body of Christ at this moment all over the earth. It has to do with the Last Harvest:

> *For thus saith the LORD of hosts; Yet once, it is a little while, and I will shake the heavens, and the earth, and the sea, and the dry land; and I will shake all nations, and the desire of all nations shall come: and I will fill this house with glory, saith the LORD of hosts (Haggai 2:6-7 KJV).*

God Himself promises, "I will fill this house with glory." Hallelujah, but the next verse seems odd to mention in this contest. It does not say that because of the glory, healing would happen, demons would flee, and revival would break out, although all that takes place when His glory comes in. God's attention is on the following:

> *The silver is mine, and the gold is mine, saith the LORD of hosts (Haggai 2:8 KJV).*

Then, God continues the previous thought:

> *The glory of the latter house shall be greater than of the former, saith the LORD of hosts: and in this place will I give peace, saith the LORD of hosts (Haggai 2:9 KJV).*

Why does God speak about glory and finances at the same time? We're all awaiting the coming of the Great Revival and the Last Harvest. The Last Harvest will happen throughout all nations and all over the earth. The Scripture says:

> *My house will be called a house of prayer for all nations (Mark 11:17).*

Throughout the history of the Church, there have been revivals that have ignited in different places and times. However, these revivals have often fizzled out due to a lack of financial support, among other reasons. It's sad that the work of God could be hindered by something as mundane as money.

The bottom line is—salvation is free. Bringing the gospel to all people of all nations is not free. We need a significant amount of resources for the Kingdom of God. The church doesn't just need some resources; we need ALL the resources to spread the Kingdom of God throughout the earth.

When God blesses you, it's not to fill your bank account but to empower you to fulfill your purpose as a son or daughter of God. Through His lordship, God teaches us to be obedient in our finances and with our sacrifices. He says, "The silver is Mine, and the gold is Mine. I will provide all resources for My Church, and the Last Harvest won't be limited due to lack of money."

Do you know why social scum and filth are increasing so much right now? Because there are wealthy people who finance these evil projects. However, before God outpours His Spirit in an unprecedented measure, He will increase finances among His people to provide for the Last Harvest. I prophesy that there will be a massive financial provision for God's people before the global revival breaks out. Before the Final Harvest, business opportunities will arise and release resources for God's people to fulfill His will on earth. Stay obedient to the Lord; you will see His favor over your life. The contracts and opportunities that seemed unreachable will become reachable. God's goodness and mercy will follow you. Remember, money is not dirty, secular, or worldly. We need all the resources for the Kingdom of God, and the glory of the latter house will be greater than the glory of the former house! Hallelujah!

Spiritual Victories Determine Physical Victories

As I write these lines, I hear the Lord saying, *In the spiritual realm, I have already freed you and all your resources. I already freed your young and old ones, your sons and daughters. I delivered you from Pharaoh — it is a finished work of Christ. Now, your part is to get it back from Pharaoh. Let no hoof remain there. I gave you silver and gold to fulfill My purpose. Start voicing My will in the physical world. Start walking in My promises. Don't give place to the devil!* The Scripture tells us that through the Cross of Jesus Christ, God has rescued us from the dominion of darkness, brought us into the kingdom of His beloved Son, and blessed us with every spiritual blessing in Christ (see Colossians 1:12-13, Ephesians 1:3). It is finished.

Do you remember when Joshua went to fight with the Amalekites, and Moses went up the mountain to pray? (see Exodus 17:8-16) Do you know why? Moses knew that spiritual victories precede physical ones. Our fight is not against flesh and blood but against principalities, powers, the rulers of the darkness of this world, and spiritual forces of evil in the heavenly places (see Ephesians 6:12). Although we walk in the flesh, we do not wage war according to the flesh. The weapons we fight with are not carnal but mighty in God to pull down strongholds. We cast down arguments and every high thing that exalts itself against the knowledge of God, bringing every thought into captivity in obedience to Christ (see 2 Corinthians 10:3-5).

Try to picture this: Moses ascends on the mountain, raises his hands to the Lord, and begins to pray and fight for the God-given promises. At the same time, his follower, his spiritual son, was fighting a war in the physical realm. When Moses held his hands up high, Joshua prevailed, but as soon as Moses lowered his hands, the enemy gained the upper hand.

God had shown me that Moses prayed from the position of victory in the spiritual realm. He prayed based on the word of God and His promise. His prayer wasn't founded on what his physical eyes saw but on the fact that God had already given Israelites the land, and they would go there with their young, old, and all their resources. Moses prayed with faith. Faith is capable of seeing the invisible. We can't always see what's happening in the spiritual world with our physical eyes. Joshua would have lost if Moses had put his hands down too early. Moses focused on the promised finished work; he endured steadfastly, keeping his eyes on the invisible One. What a spiritual position before God!

God made us a promise. Behold, the darkness shall cover the earth, and deep darkness the people. Still, *the LORD will arise over you, and His glory will be seen upon you* (Isaiah 60:2). I want all of us today to stand on the Word of God and use the authority we've been given to command every unclean spirit to get out of our houses, our children's lives, and our finances. In the spiritual realm, you are the Moses in your home. You are the Moses in your community. You've been given power and authority. Lift your voice with authority, and command every "Amalekite," every "Philistine," and every demon to get out of your children's lives, your home, your family, health, body, resources, and your generation. Do not leave a hoof behind; do not leave anything for Pharaoh. We are leaving Egypt with silver and gold and our youth, elders, and resources.

I also want to address mature believers. Understanding the magnitude of the attacks on our sons and daughters and the next generation is crucial. We can't even imagine what is happening to teenagers in today's day and age. They are confronting a multitude of struggles, enduring battles that they may not even be aware of. It's disheartening to acknowledge that some of them, as young as 12 years old, are considering committing suicide because they have either been raped, done drugs, got involved in sexual activities, have been abused, molested, bullied, or are suffering from depression and panic attacks. There is a severe spiritual war going on in their lives.

We might not understand the severity of their hardship, but here's what we can do: let's stop fighting for our traditions and forms of ministry, get on our knees, and fight for our children. To win back our sons and daughters, resources, and sacrifices. Start with your own house, your family, and your community. Command everything that didn't come from God to get out, to be gone, and never come back. God said you will tread on the lion and cobra, trample upon the young lion and the serpent. Friends, if God is for you, who can be against you? He gave you authority to trample upon the enemy. **You must voice God's Word and His promises aloud in prayer, for He fights through your mouth.**

Command with me:

> *Devil, in the mighty name of Jesus, get out of my children. Get out of my finances and home. I'm leaving the kingdom of darkness, and I'm not leaving anything behind. I choose to be under the lordship of my God. I renounce the spirit of Mammon and declare that it will no longer rule over me, dictate how and when I should serve my God, or how much I should give to the Lord. The Lord is my Shepherd; I shall not want. I will live in the shelter of the Most High, under the shadow of the Almighty. The Lord is my Refuge, my Fortress, and God in Whom I trust. Devil, you no longer have power over me. You have no authority over my children, my finances, or any other area of my life. I cancel and destroy all your plans against my life in Jesus' name. I cast you out of our house and our lives! Me and my house will serve the Lord. I worship my God and serve Him only!*

In the spiritual realm, God has already released His blessings upon your life. The blessing of the Lord enriches and does not bring sorrow with it (see Proverbs 10:22). The blessing of the Lord is more than just finances. Blessing is when we leave the spiritual Egypt and walk with our children and elders, along with our resources and sacrifices. We are walking together under the lordship of our God, under His authority, to fulfill His will here on earth as it is in heaven. Hallelujah! **Let's celebrate the Lord!**

Chapter 8
"I've Found a Man After My Own Heart"

My sheep hear My voice, and I know them, and they follow Me.

John 10:27

Month after month, I retreated to the mountains to be with God. Each time, I was full of expectation to have an encounter with Him. I envisioned coming back from that mountain with God's glory all around me, shining just like Moses. However, there were times when I would just read the Word and not feel anything. Time passed by, and I didn't receive anything. I felt so discouraged and confused, "Why am I here? God, what's going on? I've been here for three days…" Despite this, He would respond, "Son, just press on. Develop the habit. Establish discipline in your life. What I'm about to reveal to you in My Word will cost you everything, and the revelation will be heavy. I want you to continue giving yourself to Me and My word—and you will become My instrument." So, I continued.

The pillars of the secret place and the pursuit of a close relationship with God are to come to know Him intimately, hear His voice, and do what He asks you so that He might reign as the Lord of your life. People often ask me, "How can you know God personally? How can you hear His voice? How can you understand God?" The journey takes place in steps, so let's go in order.

First, you need to learn His language—fill yourself with the Word of God. Yes, this is absolutely necessary! Before God sent Ezekiel to fulfill his calling, God told the prophet:

> *And He said to me, "Son of man, feed your belly, and **fill** your stomach with this scroll that I give you." So I ate, and it was in my mouth like honey in sweetness. Then He said to me: "Son of man, go to the house of Israel and speak with My words to them" (Ezekiel 3:3-4).*

In the book of Ezekiel, God instructs the prophet to consume a "scroll," symbolizing the importance of having the Word in you. It's not enough to skim through one chapter a day on the Bible app. The Word must become part of you to the point that it fills your entire being. It requires intentional effort to get to a different level in God. You need to be intentional and start to live in the Word and fill yourself with it so that His Word will begin pushing out everything that is not of the Father in your life. So, fill yourself with the Word until it begins to speak to you and deal with your way of life and thinking, piercing to the division of soul and of spirit, of joint and of marrow, and discerning the thoughts and intentions of the heart (see Hebrew 4:12). And when the Word becomes a part of you. Ezekiel 3:4 will become a reality, and you will start to speak with His words.

In the vision, the prophet Ezekiel ate the scroll; it was sweet in his mouth like honey. If you feed yourself with the Word until it speaks to you, you will enjoy it. It won't be a burden—you will begin to desire His revelation earnestly.

Second, you need to place yourself under the teaching of the Kingdom of God. While it is commendable to study the Bible, it's not enough. Many people read and know passages of Scripture by heart, but if you don't allow the Holy Spirit to renew your mind with the message of the Kingdom, you will interpret God's words incorrectly. Based on my observations, it appears that when God commissions a person, He wants to deal with their mindset. Why? So they won't add their own words, opinions, and experiences, and they won't take away from His Words when they carry His message, but instead, they would reflect His will and speak His words. That's why it is essential to be under Kingdom teaching and understand its message.

To be in His Presence

I want to warn you against one extreme. See, a lot of people believe that coming to God's presence is the goal. The main thing. Not exactly. When Jesus taught about the lordship of God, He didn't just emphasize coming to His presence; He pointed out three critical elements: coming, hearing, and doing. Luke 6:46-48 says:

> *But why do you call Me 'Lord, Lord,' and not do the things which I say? Whoever **comes** to Me, and **hears** My sayings and **does** them, I will show you whom he is like: He is like a man building a house, who dug deep and laid the foundation on the rock.*

Just because you pray and God answers your prayers does not mean He's the Lord of your life. Just because you feel His presence does not make Him the Lord of your life. Many people go to church, worship God, and call Him Lord. They sing songs about it. But this doesn't mean that He is their Lord. Many people have received salvation but never learned to surrender and live under God's complete lordship.

Let's examine the three critical things Jesus discussed when He talked about the lordship of God: *coming, hearing, and doing.*

Coming

Please do not take one word out of context and take it to extremes. Many preachers do that, saying that the most important thing is being in the presence of God, loving God, and worshiping Him. This is important, and I won't argue with that. However, for some believers, their Christian lifestyle has transformed into a constant pursuit of attending conferences solely to experience His presence. Would you want your child always to come and only talk about their love for you and never do anything else? Picture this kind of relationship.

Say my teenage son comes to me, sits on my lap, and says, "Daddy, I love you." Naturally, I would reply, "Yes, I love you too, son." But I can't just sit and talk about love forever. I would eventually get up to attend to other things that I have to do. Now let's say my son follows me, waiting to sit close to me again and talk about his love for me. But life is not just about sitting next to me and professing love. Do you see my point? In this scenario, I would tell him, "Well, if you love me, son, please help me with a few tasks. I have big plans. I have big dreams. I have a lot to accomplish. Can I count on you?" Then he would reply, "Dad, what are you talking about? I only need to be in your presence and tell you how much I love you." *Where did we get these extremes?*

Why do I bring this up? Because Jesus also spoke about this in the parable of the two sons. The father told his sons, "Please, go and work today in my vineyard." The first son said he wouldn't go but then repented and went. The second son promised to go but never did. Jesus concluded with a question, "Which of the two did the will of his father?" (see Matthew 21:28-31).

Imagine if Jesus was a part of this extreme and loved His Father so much that He didn't leave the throne room. Yet, Jesus said from the beginning: *"Here I am… I have come to do your will, my God"* (see Hebrews 10:7 NIV). We should follow His example! We must not only **come** to the presence of God but **hear** His voice and then go and **do** His will. In the book of Isaiah, chapter 6, the prophet heard the cry of God while he was in His presence: *"Who shall I send? And who will go for Us?"* (Isaiah 6:8). Who will go and do the will of the Father?

It's essential not only to come to God's presence but to live from His presence.

Hearing

The next element is hearing. It is written: *"and hears My sayings"* (see Luke 6:46-48). *Hearing* happens when God begins to share His thoughts and when the Word speaks to you. We come to Him to hear His voice. Turns out, the goal of the secret place isn't to pray really hard for a couple of hours. The goal of the secret place is to know Him and hear His voice. It can be for an hour, a whole day, three days, or even a week that you separate and devote to Him. However, coming to His presence and being alone with God for an extended time doesn't make Him your Lord either.

How many people today hear from God and "collect" prophecies and revelations? They follow anointed men and women of God and listen to their sermons but don't do or change anything in their lives. Why would God speak to us or place ministering gifts in the body of Christ? So that we would just collect prophecies and revelations? Unfortunately, I've encountered many Christians who heard revelations about God's lordship and His will for them, but they didn't fulfill His call. If we don't take practical steps, everything will stay as head knowledge—we will never see the manifestation of His lordship in our lives. The scariest thing is that many hear His voice and know the will of God for them but do nothing. Remember, it's essential to hear the Word and do what the Father entrusted us to do. He is expecting obedience from us.

Doing

We are the sons and daughters of the Kingdom. In the epistle to the Colossians 1:13, it is written:

He has delivered us from the power of darkness and conveyed us into the kingdom of the Son of His love.

God has already delivered us from the kingdom of darkness and brought us into the kingdom of His Son. This extraordinary feat has been accomplished, granting us the ability to live in this world without being bound by its systems. Instead, we find ourselves under the lordship of God. Jesus perfectly demonstrated that way of life. He lived under the complete lordship of God. That is why religious structures and political systems were left frustrated and powerless in their attempts to control and manipulate Jesus; He relied solely on the authority of God. **He was in the world but remained untainted by the world, all because He submitted Himself fully to the lordship of God and His Kingdom.**

In today's Christianity, we've mixed too many cultural elements with Kingdom culture, which is the reason we don't see God's lordship on earth. Most of us grew up in a democratic society and, as a result, have the tendency to apply the same approach in our churches. Nowadays, some churches have adopted a voting system similar to political parties, where members elect their leadership and vote on resolutions and amendments to the constitution and the law. I want to tell you that this approach doesn't exist in the Kingdom of God. There is one King in the Kingdom, and His Word is final. There is no room for arguments about His Words, will, ways, or voting when it comes to implementation. As believers, we are called to submit to His Word. He is the King and the Lord of everything.

Do you understand that from the beginning, God's plan was for His people to be set apart and ruled by Him alone? His plan was for God Himself to rule over Israel. However, the Israelites rejected that and asked for a human king so that they would be like other nations. They wanted to be like everyone else and voted for a king to lead and rule over them. But God wanted to be King over Israel and govern His people through prophets and judges.

Today, in Christianity, the process of selecting pastors has taken a different form. But, in God's Kingdom, pastors aren't voted in. The Bible says that God has appointed apostles, prophets, evangelists, pastors, teachers, and ministers (see 1 Corinthians 12:28). It's God Who chooses and appoints these ministers. There is a great danger when people elect and appoint ministers over themselves; sooner or later, those ministers will be ensnared in the trap of pleasing people rather than God.

Let me clarify: We can only acknowledge and affirm pastors when we see God's calling on their lives; only then can church elders lay hands on them and ordain them. We shouldn't choose ministers ourselves. This is God's church, and this is His Kingdom. If we start choosing pastors, we'll judge by what our eyes see and what our ears hear. Then, down the road, these ministers will be tempted to appeal to people and please the people who chose them.

That's what happened to King Saul. During his reign, he experienced a significant change of behavior that altered his destiny. He began to prioritize the opinions and influence of the people, ultimately drifting him away from the path that pleased God. His heart gradually lost sight of God's will. Consequently, Saul took the deadly path of compromise, a path that led him further away from God.

Obedience is Better than Sacrifice

In the book of Samuel, God commanded Saul:

> *Samuel also said to Saul, "The LORD sent me to anoint you king over His people, over Israel. Now therefore, heed the voice of the words of the LORD. Thus says the Lord of hosts: 'I will punish Amalek for what he did to Israel, how he ambushed him on the way when he came up from Egypt. Now go and attack Amalek, and utterly destroy all that they have, and do not spare them (1 Samuel 15:1-3).*

Thus, God gave King Saul a task and expected him to fulfill the word of the Lord. Saul didn't fully do what God asked Him to do. He compromised, leaving the oxen and the best of the livestock. Then he tried to justify himself by saying that he was planning to give them to the Lord as burnt offerings.

The question naturally arises:

"But did God ask you to do that?"

Look what it says further in verse 22:

> *So Samuel said: "Has the LORD as great delight in burnt offerings and sacrifices, as in obeying the voice of the LORD? Behold, to obey is better than sacrifice, and to heed than the fat of rams..." (1 Samuel 15:22).*

Friend, I know we can sacrifice and do a lot of things for God. We can dedicate our finances, time, and talents to different projects and ministries. Understand this: **you can sacrifice much and never please God.** You can be a part of some ministry, go on mission trips, and do projects in the local church, but never fulfill God's will for you. Do you really think that sacrifice is more delightful to God than obedience to the voice of the Holy Spirit?

We need to learn to *come* to Him, to *hear* Him, and to *do* what He speaks to us wholeheartedly. And every Christian should be led by the Holy Spirit within us, not by the opinion of others.

The most important thing in our relationship with God is obedience to His Word. And thankfully, He gives us the grace to fulfill His Word according to the measure of the gift of Christ in us. Unfortunately, some of us are acting like Jonah, running from God's voice. As humans, we tend to avoid responsibilities. Later on, we try to make up and justify ourselves with our sacrifices to God. Yes, you can tithe, help the poor, serve in the church, and comfort yourself with the thought that you are doing so much for God! And yet, despite sacrificing and serving as much as possible, you still might never fulfill your original calling, thus never pleasing God. It all comes down to the ultimate act of devotion that God seeks: willingly surrendering on the altar and declaring, "From this moment on, it's not my will to be done. It's Yours, God. Not my dreams be done, but Yours."

Once God redeemed every one of us and positioned us in His Kingdom. He pulled us from the kingdom of darkness and into the Kingdom of Light, making us His children, a royal priesthood. These aren't just phrases in the Scripture. He has a purpose for each of us in His Kingdom. A specific calling is given to every single person. And God expects something from us.

That's why I'm emphasizing this truth over and over again. You can sacrifice much and never please God. You can have a successful ministry and serve in a church yet never fulfill your purpose and God-given calling.

You may ask:

"Isn't ministry my calling? And the more we minister, the better?"

"Did you hear that from Him?"

The Scripture emphasizes, "...*be filled with the knowledge of His will*" (Colossians 1:9). You need to listen to Him to get to know His will for your life and be led by the Holy Spirit. When I begin to understand His will for me and start fulfilling it, I have an inner witness, the Holy Spirit, telling me that I'm walking worthy of the call of God, pleasing Him in everything.

Sacrifices attract human attention, but obedience attracts God's attention.

Saul failed to heed the word of the Lord because his heart wasn't devoted to God Himself. He dedicated himself to serving God, neglecting a deeper connection with Him. He was more concerned with people's opinions. Regrettably, his priorities were distorted, and he prioritized the approval of his fellow men over God's will.

Then God said, "Enough. I will find a man **after My own heart**, who will do all **My** will."

The Difference Between Saul and David

Do you know the difference between the reigns of David and Saul? Acts 2:25 says:

> *For David says concerning Him: 'I foresaw the* **Lord** *always before my face, For He is at my right hand, that I may not be shaken.'*

In other words, David held his gaze on the Lord and submitted himself under His lordship. Allow me to reiterate: **from the beginning, David's attention was on the Lord.**

When David battled against Goliath, his brothers said, "Who do you think you are? We know your prideful heart." But at that moment, David wasn't prideful; he remained very humble before God. And when David said, "Who is this uncircumcised Philistine," he wasn't speaking out of pride or arrogance. This kind of boldness to face the giant was the result of a close relationship with the Lord. Yet, in the eyes of his brothers, it seemed like pride.

David valued closeness with the Holy Spirit so much that nothing else held a higher value for him to take his attention away. As you know, **your attention will always be on things you value the most.** David didn't fear losing his kingdom or reputation. He cared about it, but it wasn't his main priority. Let's read his prayer to God after he sinned:

> *Against You, You only, have I sinned, And done this evil in Your sight... Create in me a clean heart, O God, and renew a steadfast spirit within me. Do not cast me away from Your presence, and* **do not take Your Holy Spirit from me** *(Psalm 51:4, 10-13).*

David's plea to God was heartfelt. He said, "And do not take Your Holy Spirit from me." This means David was connected with the Holy Spirit and was scared to lose Him. Through all his drama and challenges, David was utterly worried and kept his focus on maintaining his closeness with God's Spirit. He deeply cared about his fellowship with God. His biggest fear was losing God's voice in his life, His presence.

And later (verse 14), in his prayer of repentance, he says: *"Restore to me the joy of Your salvation, and uphold me by Your generous Spirit."* (Russian Synodal Bible translation says, *uphold me by* **Your Spirit of lordship**) This speaks of God's lordship! In other words, David was crying out: "God, establish Your lordship in my life once again."

After repenting, let me summarize what David asked God for:

First, do not take your Holy Spirit from me.

Second, affirm Your lordship in my life.

Allow me to draw your attention to the moment God turned away from Saul. What I find interesting is that God did not reject Saul from ruling over the kingdom of Israel. In fact, Saul continued to reign for an impressive 32 years! So, what exactly did God reject Saul from? He withdrew His lordship from Saul. The Spirit of the Lord departed from him, as it is written in 1 Samuel 16:14. God removed His lordship and transferred it to someone else, leaving Saul without His presence.

Saul continued to rule over Israel, but he began to suffer. He stopped hearing God. God no longer answered or guided him. Although Saul still held onto his crown, his talents, his position, and all the wealth and responsibilities that came with being king, something crucial was missing from his life. He no longer heard God's voice or felt His presence. The Spirit of the LORD was absent, and Saul was left without God's lordship. It's reminiscent of the story of Adam, who, through his disobedience, also rejected God's lordship over his life.

"I've Found A Man After My Own Heart"

The Spirit of the Lord rested upon David, and God said this about him, "I've found a man after My own heart, who will do all My will" (see Acts 13:22). Essentially, God was saying, "I have found a person who pursues My heart and My desires. **I've found someone after My own heart** who will do everything I ask of him, which is why I will lead him in paths of righteousness for My name's sake. I will be his Lord and his Shepherd. He will live under My lordship."

Yes, David was far from perfect; he made mistakes and sinned, but he was considered a man after God's heart. How come? Well, God looks at everything completely different than we do. I'm not excusing David's wrongdoings but highlighting what made him special in God's eyes. David's priorities were to hear the voice of God and have closeness with the Holy Spirit. David treasured God's voice, His word, and his relationship with the Holy Spirit so much that this devotion allowed God to work through David to fulfill His plan on earth.

At the end of David's life, his last speech to the assembly of people was a testament to his deep personal experiential knowledge of God and his unwavering heart:

Therefore David blessed the LORD before all the assembly; and David said:

> "*Blessed are You, LORD God of Israel, our Father, forever and ever. Yours, O LORD, is the greatness, the power and the glory, the victory and the majesty; for all that is in heaven and in earth is Yours; Yours is the kingdom, O LORD, and You are exalted as head over all. Both riches and honor come from You, and You reign over all. In Your hand is power and might; in Your hand it is to make great and to give strength to all. "Now therefore, our God, we thank You and praise* **Your glorious name**" *(1 Chronicles 29:10-13).*

What is that name? *LORD*.

That's the difference: Saul ruled himself, but David allowed God to rule through him.

Remember, God does not become our Lord just because we call Him Lord in our prayers. Only if we obey His words and heed His leading is His lordship activated in our lives. Conversely, if we don't obey, we push away His lordship from our lives. It's that simple.

Obedience

Jesus was obedient to God in everything, even unto death on the cross (see Philippians 2:6-9). There is a level of obedience to God that requires you to die to yourself. He gave us an example of what this life of obedience looks like: "the Son can do nothing of Himself, but what He sees the Father do."

I relentlessly seek His face, His voice, and His leading even in the little things so that I may reach a point where it's no longer I who live, but Christ lives through me.

What activates His lordship in your life? It's none other than obedience. It is written:

> *Blessed rather are those who hear the word of God and obey it (Luke 11:28 NIV).*

Let me repeat it: **Every time I submit to God and obey His Word, I activate His lordship in my life.** Here's a practical example of what this looks like. The Bible says: *"Pray for those who spitefully use you and persecute you"* (Matthew 5:44). You might read it a hundred times, but if you don't do it, this Word of God doesn't become a part of you. Activate the lordship of God in your life by praying for those who have offended you.

In general, I call Matthew chapters 5,6 and 7 the constitution of the Kingdom of God. These chapters are the foundation for growing in obedience and living out the fulfillment of His Word; this is where we need to start. I constantly re-read the 5th, 6th, and 7th chapters of Matthew. There, Jesus shows how to open the door to God's lordship in every area of our lives. Just imagine for a moment: we can live a life that pleases God in everything we do—a life of total obedience and submission to His lordship. Such people are dangerous to the kingdom of darkness.

Remember, the measure of God's lordship in your life is proportional to your obedience to Him. Your obedience to the voice of God will keep you in the will of God. Your obedience to the voice of God will determine the extent to which you fulfill your purpose here on earth.

Your obedience to God will determine the measure of His lordship in your life and the level of His glory released through you on earth.

Eternity is a Lot Closer

Fight for your relationship with God. Take your eyes off all the vanity. Don't be conformed to this world, but present your body as a living sacrifice (see Romans 12:1-2). Friend, learn to **come** to Him, **hear** Him, and **do** what He tells you. Lift your eyes to the heavens where your help comes from. Stop comforting yourself with your many sacrifices and offerings. Don't just go through the motions of serving in the church and doing good deeds for others. Instead, be eager to listen to God's voice and to know the assignment He has for you, then fulfill it. Remember, obedience is more important than sacrifice. The sad truth is that when we ignore God's commands, we cut ourselves off from His lordship. I pray that the Lord will help you live in complete obedience to Him.

We often say, "I want to be a person after God's heart." And we think that if we pray more, we will be after God's heart. Or, if we fast and sacrifice more, we will be after God's heart. All that is important, but it's not the proper perspective. More prayer doesn't equate to being after the heart of God. Instead of repeating, "I want to be a person after God's heart," let's examine our hearts and lives. Is God really the Lord of your life in everything?

I've had a few out-of-body experiences in my life. While in the physical body, all our senses are dulled, and some memories fade. When a person leaves the body, their memory, feelings, and emotions intensify exponentially. They remember everything with astonishing clarity—every situation, every conversation, every deed, and every feeling and emotion intertwined with them. Every circumstance and instance remains in their memory.

Why am I even mentioning this? See, many believers who lived out their God-given time on earth will be in heaven and will remember every opportunity, every chance, and every moment God gave them to

"I've Found a Man After My Own Heart"

do something, but they ignored it. He was calling them to go further in knowing Him. He was waiting for them in the secret place. He was waking them up at night to pray. But they lived for themselves. And the most challenging thing will be to be there in eternity and understand that you didn't do what you were supposed to with your time on earth. In other words, you missed the mark. You attracted people's attention with your donations, gifts, service, programs, and sacrifices, doing what was pleasing in people's eyes. You have lived what appears to be a good Christian life, but you never fulfilled your purpose. You're saved, but you didn't fulfill God's calling for your life. This is tragic.

Consider this: If you have not established a strong relationship with God during your time on earth, do you really think you'll suddenly become close to Him in eternity? No, there will be different levels of glory in eternity. If you did not prioritize Him as a Person while on earth, and the desires of His heart were not your prime concern, why do you think you'll suddenly be close to Him in eternity? Just because you prayed and God answered your prayers doesn't mean you were close to Him. Just because you had a ministry doesn't mean you were close to Him. Just because you sacrificed doesn't mean you were close to Him. In the end, the level of glory and closeness with Jesus will differ for each of us. So, it is important to ask yourself: Where is your focus now? What is the current state of your relationship with Him?

As I write this chapter, my heart cries to the heavens, "God, I have no desire to pursue my own plans or build my ministry. I'm here on earth for one thing—I want to fulfill Your will. I long to know You. I want to hear Your voice. I will obey. Guide me. Draw me closer to You, align my heart with Yours, and empower me to fulfill Your purpose for my life."

In today's world, we can radically live for Christ. I believe we can live under the complete lordship of God. Amidst the chaos of these last days, among all the global catastrophes, wars and rumors of wars, political turmoil, and financial instability, it is the lordship of God that will shield and protect us. **I absolutely believe we can live in this world but be like Jesus and not conform to its systems because we submit to the lordship of God.** And just like Him, we will also spread God's Kingdom and be a blessing to all people.

I firmly believe that what was happening in Jesus' life and ministry is accessible to us, too. I'm passionate about seeing the extraordinary events of the book of Acts unfold in this generation and God's glory being manifested. That lifestyle won't just come out of hearing the revelation; it will come out of our obedience.

After you finish this book, I don't want to hear about how many new things you learned. I really want to hear what you began to practice in your life, how your relationship with God changed, and how you came to know Him, hear Him, and do what He tells you to do.

> *Lord, I pray right now for the one reading this book. Holy Spirit, touch this person. Allow this woman or man to see their lives from an eternal perspective. Give them the opportunity to pause and listen to Your voice. Give them the strength to change what needs to be changed. Give them a hunger and desire to know and understand Your will and to bring forth the things in the body of Christ that You expect from them. Lead them further, Holy Spirit. May they become Your disciples, people after Your heart, and may they **fulfill** all Your desires for them.*

In the mighty name of Jesus Christ. Amen.

Chapter 9
The Breath Of God

But the hour is coming, and now is, when the true worshipers will worship the Father in spirit and truth; for the Father is seeking such to worship Him.

John 4:23

It's not always easy to talk about your flaws and mistakes, or when you've missed the mark and had to repent and ask forgiveness. But I promised you from the beginning of this book that I would be open and not only share my victories but my mistakes too, and what God taught me throughout these many years, restoring me into sonship and as His messenger on earth. Here we go.

At the beginning of last year, I canceled everything again and went to the mountains to be alone with the Lord. I began to pray, "God, what's going on with me? I'm not the same as I was before. I don't want to pretend. I want to be real before You, myself, and those around me. God, I feel stuck. I feel lukewarm…"

Visibly, everything was going great: the church was expanding, the ministry was acquiring momentum, the team was growing, and different departments within the ministry were developing, too. I ministered and preached a lot; the anointing was operating powerfully, and people were encountering God. But deep inside, I felt like I had a lid on. It's as if I couldn't break through and go further in God. Finding the right words to describe that inner condition is hard, but it seemed like my personal relationship with God was stagnant. It wasn't noticeable to others, but I recognized the subtle shift within me.

So, I took a fast and went to the mountains, wholeheartedly praying, "God, something changed in my relationship with You. I feel I've become lukewarm. No one notices it, but I do! God, I don't want You to stop breathing on my life. I want to go further in You! Holy Spirit, test my heart, show me what's going on with me."

I heard His voice, "Do you really want to know?"

"Yes, I want to know. Teach me, Holy Spirit."

"Son, pride is in your life. It hinders you and slows Me down."

"Pride? How so? Where? In what?"

As I sat there, the Holy Spirit reminded me of instances where I disregarded others, responded condescendingly, or sought my interests. I felt ashamed and upset that these attitudes still lived in my heart.

The Holy Spirit continued:

"You talk a lot from the pulpit about how much you humble yourself. You didn't even notice that, at some point, you started preaching more about yourself and less about Me. You start using too much "me" and "I" in your messages. Son, I didn't call you to talk about humility; I called you to walk in humility. Humility isn't talked about; humility is walked in. And when you're walking in humility, you talk about My glory, My works, and My goodness."

Instantly, I was on my face before God, "Forgive me, Lord! I don't want to be this way. I don't want to be prideful. I don't want to be great in my own eyes. God, forgive me! I'll fix everything. I'll ask these people for forgiveness. Forgive me, Holy Spirit. I feel so ashamed that such impurities still have a place in my heart. Help me to be humble and compassionate like Jesus. God, give me the strength to reflect Your nature. Transform me, God; I surrender myself to You." In a moment, I felt God's presence rushing over me like a river. I sensed His fresh anointing. His breath upon me! Finally! Friend, this experience was priceless!

God, Bring Your Order

Scripture tells us that God opposes the proud but gives grace to the humble (see James 4:6). He sees everything inside us. He has complete knowledge of what's going on in our hearts at all times. If pride is in your life, God will get in your way. Not the devil, but God Himself will confront your arrogance. Despite your efforts to pray, intercede, declare, command, and bind all spiritual forces, you will not succeed because you're not coming against the devil but against God.

It's clear that God wants to lead each and every one of us toward a **deeper** relationship with Him, His truth, His knowledge, and His divine revelation. However, the question remains: *How much do we truly want it? How open are we to change?* Being gentle and respectful, the Holy Spirit will never force you; instead, He will reveal the obstacles that hinder you from going further in God. Ultimately, the rest is your decision; it's between you and God. It is your life, and you must make the conscious decision to walk this path.

Sometimes, we don't understand ourselves or what lies within us. That is why it's essential to have the courage to pray as David did: *"Search me, O God, and know my heart; Try me, and know my anxieties; And see if there is any wicked way in me, and lead me in the way everlasting"* (Psalm 139:23-24). Yes, this is a bold prayer and the right one if you want to be close to God! In fact, asking God to test your heart is the best thing you can do to pursue God's heart.

Let me say it again, "Test my heart, examine my thoughts, search if there is any wicked or offensive way in me, and lead me in the way of righteousness." This is the ultimate prayer for the one who wants to be after the heart of God.

As believers, we want God to bring order to our churches, ministries, families, and relationships. But the key is to let Him start with ourselves. Allow God to begin with our personal lives and bring order to our thoughts, motives, emotions, hearts, and relationships. Just realize that in the end, we won't be held accountable by our pastors, parents, mentors, or friends. It is God Himself who will judge us. So, if He's the One who awaits us at the end, let's strive to walk before Him, live according to His ways, and allow Him to change us and guide us into His perfect will.

Why Uzziah?

There is an account in the Bible where the prophet Isaiah beheld the spiritual realm and witnessed the Lord sitting on His throne. This extraordinary account is vividly described by the prophet, who writes these words:

In the year that King Uzziah died, I saw the LORD sitting on a throne, high and lifted up... (Isaiah 6:1).

The prophet Isaiah saw the Lord. But what does King Uzziah have to do with Isaiah seeing *the LORD sitting on the throne high and lifted up?* Why was Uzziah mentioned in the same sentence? Recording King Uzziah's death was not a mere coincidence. Every phrase in this prophetic book is purposeful.

King Uzziah was known for his prideful nature. Initially, he was a good king and did right in the sight of the Lord, and God Himself favored him. However, as Uzziah's power and fame expanded, so did his arrogance. Uzziah didn't just become prideful; he started to infringe upon the priesthood. Look what is written about him in 2 Chronicles 26:16 (NLT):

> *But when he had become powerful, he also became proud, which led to his downfall. He sinned against the LORD his God by entering the sanctuary of the LORD's Temple and personally burning incense on the incense altar.*

Uzziah's heart swelled with pride, and God took notice! In the book of Proverbs, chapter 6, it lists seven abominations that God hates. You might ask, "Is God not love? How can God hate?" Yes, He can and He does. The first item on the list is haughty or proud eyes (see Proverbs 6:16-17 NIV). Why the eyes, you may ask? The eyes are the windows of our temple or body, and they reveal how you see the world and everyone in it. With your eyes you perceive things and act accordingly. See, when you judge a person, maybe you don't fully realize it, but in judging someone else, you are elevating yourself above them in some way. It's a sign of prideful eyes. If you envy, it means you don't see God rightly. Criticism, complaining, judging, unforgiveness, and envy are rooted in prideful eyes. God hates pride and resists it. For it is written: *"Every mountain and hill shall be made low… rough ground shall become level, the rugged places a plain. And the glory of the LORD shall be revealed"* (Isaiah 40:4-5 NIV). In other words, the glory of God can't be revealed until the mountain of pride in our life is made low.

Let's return to the book of Isaiah and closely examine the text:

> *In the year that King Uzziah died, I saw the LORD sitting on a throne, high and lifted up, and the train of His robe filled the temple.*
>
> *Above it stood seraphim; each one had six wings: with two he covered his face, with two he covered his feet, and with two he flew (Isaiah 6:1-2).*

When pride died in the land, and the mountain was made low, the prophet saw the Lord sitting on the throne, high and lifted up, noticing that no one was higher than Him.

It's not just a narrative; the prophet Isaiah described the spiritual realm and revealed the blueprint of how God's lordship is orchestrated. First, let's talk about the way worship is happening in Heaven. Who is the center of worship? What is everyone focusing on? Are the musicians, the pastor, and the instruments the center of attention? Is the worship leader the central figure? No. Everyone's attention is on Him in heaven, and everything revolves around Him. Even the seraphim covered their faces to not draw attention to themselves. Everything must revolve around Him, the One Who is above all, high and lifted up, the Ruler of all.

> *And one cried to another and said: "Holy, holy, holy is the LORD of hosts; The whole earth is full of His glory!" (Isaiah 6:3).*

Shouldn't we do the same? When we worship together, we're not just singing to each other. Not at all! We're all coming into agreement with the words proclaiming His holiness, "Holy, holy, holy, is the Lord God Almighty!" Through this proclamation, something begins to stir in the spiritual realm.

When we exalt Him with all our hearts, minds, and strength, and when our words of adoration are focused on Him and all the worship is centered on Him—His glory fills the room. **When our worship reaches heaven, His glory manifests on earth.** For it is written: "The whole earth is full of His glory." Whenever we focus on Him and magnify His name in worship, it is impossible for nothing to happen on earth and in our lives. This way of surrendering to worship Him affirms His lordship and releases His glory in our lives!

Let's read what happens next:

And the posts of the door were shaken by the voice of him who cried out, and the house was filled with smoke (Isaiah 6:4).

Notice that there is no whispering, silence, or shyness in heaven's worship. *Their voices caused the posts of the door of the Temple to shake.* This is how loudly they worshiped the Lord, with no one mumbling their praises. I want to dedicate this passage in Scripture to those who oppose loud worship. Friends, let's strive to worship on earth as it is in heaven, **the way it pleases Him.**

Unfortunately, some believers say, "I won't go to this church/conference because the worship is too loud, and I don't like their worship." Hold on, who are they worshiping? You? Are they supposed to adjust worship for you to like it? Since when do you get to personally judge worship? What do you have to do with it?

Again, in heaven, they didn't whisper their praises. The sound of their worship shook the whole Temple! Hallelujah! Therefore, the strength of your voice with which you praise God matters. What happened next?

The entire house was filled with smoke. In the New Testament, this house represents us—we are the temple of the Holy Spirit. The house of God should not be filled with discouragement, fear, sadness, depression, and silence. God's house should be overflowing with worship and His manifested Shekinah glory. I firmly believe God is leading His Church toward a future where His glory and power will fill every corner, making us unshakable in the midst of great shaking, and nothing unclean will be able to withstand us.

Acknowledging His lordship through worship is more than just singing a song. It's a powerful declaration of submission to His authority. When all your attention in worship is focused on honoring the Lord, transformation occurs that even the devil fears.

Your Attention Determines Your Worship

Your worship is linked to God's lordship in your life. It's evident from the start of Jesus' ministry that He had to address the topic of worship. That is why Lucifer took Jesus up to a high mountain:

> *Then the devil, taking Him up on a high mountain, showed Him all the kingdoms of the world in a moment in time.*
>
> *And the devil said to Him, "All this authority I will give You, and their glory; for this has been delivered to me, and I give it to whomever I wish..." (Luke 4:5-6).*

Really quick: This conversation happened before the Cross. Yes, before the Cross, the devil had authority, but after Jesus' death and resurrection, this authority was stripped away from him (see Matthew 28:18).

Let's examine the tactics of the devil. On a high mountain, he showed Jesus all the kingdoms of this world and their splendor. Remember the third chapter of Genesis, in Eden, when Eve was enticed by the fruit and the serpent's cunning words, she lost sight of God's words. A similar strategy was used on that mountain. In a moment, the adversary showed Jesus all the kingdoms of the world and said, "Behold this splendor! The authority, the power, the glory, all this will be Yours. Shift your focus away from Your Father. Take your attention from the Lord. Just for a moment, forget what lies beyond. Focus your attention here. All this will be Yours. Marvel at the magnificence of the world."

It's hard not to wonder, "Lucifer, why so generous all of a sudden? Why are you ready to give up all these kingdoms, with all their glory and splendor? What could be worth more for you?" This means that whatever Lucifer is about to say holds greater value than any kingdom, its glory, and its power. As it reads:

Therefore, if You will worship before me, all will be Yours (Luke 4:7).

Have we fully grasped the essence of worship? After all, Lucifer was ready to give up everything he had to be worshiped. He didn't ask Jesus to sing him a song. When the subject of worship was raised, there was no grand stage, instruments, songbooks, or drums. The true nature of worship transcends all those trivial things people often debate about.

Also, some theologians say that Lucifer was the worship leader in heaven. I'm not sure where they got that idea. The Scripture says he was an anointed Cherub (see Ezekiel 28:14). Cherubim are revealed as the carriers and protectors of God's presence (see Psalm 18:10). The Word says that God rode upon a cherub. In his time, Lucifer was the head of all the other cherubim. He had the closest position to God. He knew God's glory, power, and authority well because he was carrying His glory (see Ezekiel 28:14, where one of the meanings of the word *covers* is to carry). Eventually, Lucifer switched his focus from God to his own beauty and anointing, craving attention for himself. This instance marked the turning point where his connection with God's breath was forever severed. Please don't miss this: He ceased to prioritize the Lord and instead sought worship for himself.

It is written:

> *Your heart was lifted up because of your beauty; you corrupted your wisdom for the sake of your splendor (Ezekiel 28:17).*

Here we find the main reason satan was cast out of heaven. It's a warning to all of us: When people start to operate in the anointing and power of God (to this day, this is a reality for many ministers), at some point, they may start to look at themselves, their achievements, the size of their ministry, their popularity, revelations, and anointing, not noticing that they're taking credit for God's glory. And as soon as pride creeps in, stagnation and failure follow closely behind. *My God, protect us from this! Protect Your ministers!*

Pride draws attention to itself. Humility keeps the attention on the Lord.

> *And Jesus answered and said to him, "Get behind me, Satan! For it is written, 'You shall worship the Lord your God, and Him only you shall serve'" (Luke 4:8).*

You shall worship the Lord your God! The devil knows **where your attention lies; that is where your worship will be.** The act of worship determines your lordship and confirms your submission to His authority.

An important thing to recognize in this verse is the order of words. First, *worship the Lord,* and then *Him only you shall serve.* Therefore, no matter what kind of ministry or work you do, worship comes first. Ministry should come from your worship, not vice versa. **Your ministry must follow your worship of the Lord!**

I believe that God is restoring true worship all over the face of the earth. On earth as it is in heaven. The Father is looking for worshippers who will worship Him in spirit and truth so His will would be done on earth as in heaven (see John 4:23).

Don't forget that when all your attention is on the Lord, then His attention will be on you.

God is Restoring True Worship

In Acts 15 says:

> *And with this the words of the prophets agree, just as it is written: "After this, I will return and will rebuild the tabernacle of David, which has fallen down; I will rebuild its ruins, and I will set it up..." (Acts 15:15-16).*

In other words, God says, "I still remember the Tabernacle of David, who in his time understood something that was in My heart..." In the previous chapter, we discussed how David's connection with the Spirit of God influenced his approach to worship. By faith, David introduced a new dimension to worship, something that didn't yet exist in the minds of humanity. Imagine David's life! This was a time when people offered goats, calves, and other animals as sacrifices and acts of worship to God, the shedding of animal blood was a common occurrence. And here came David standing amidst these established rituals, opinions, traditional practices, and forms. He dared to embrace his musical talent, composing new songs dedicated to the Lord, engaging in dance, and gathering with like-minded, passionate people who shared his fervor for worship, proclaiming what true worship is here on earth as it is in heaven.

During his life, David understood the heart of worship and created the right atmosphere for the glory of God to descend on earth. God breathed on David's worship, and there heaven and earth connected. God's desire for worship is evident in those words spoken through the prophets, "I will rebuild once again the Tabernacle of David which has fallen down." The word rebuild implies that it was once there but was destroyed. Rebuilding doesn't mean creating something new; it means restoring what once was.

God doesn't force people to worship Him. True worship stems from an intimate revelation of who God is. He enlightens those who seek Him and are hungry for Him. He's leading His Church into a state where He can restore true worship, the Tabernacle of David. Heaven will once again begin to unite with earth, and God's glory will descend.

The next verse tells us why God wants to restore it:

So that the rest of mankind may seek the LORD, even all the Gentiles who are called by My name, says the LORD who does all these things (Acts 15:17).

Yes, David built the Tabernacle of worship in Israel. However, the Seed of David gave every nation, tribe, and tongue access to this Tabernacle. Today, God is reviving this connection across the whole earth. The name of the LORD will be exalted in every nation and language! People from every corner of the world, every culture, every tongue, and every nationality will come together and worship as one, in spirit and in truth. We'll all cry out in unison, "Worthy! Worthy! Worthy! All the praise is Yours. All the glory is Yours. All the worship is Yours!"

God says, "I will rebuild the Tabernacle of David to restore sonship in My house so that every person can encounter Me there. I will inhabit the earth with heaven's glory."

Here Comes the Older Brother

I can almost guarantee that there will always be an older brother saying, "I'm not coming!" In the first chapters of this book, we talked about God's desire to adopt people and restore everything. Let's revisit the parable of the prodigal son (see Luke 15:11-32). There, we see how Jesus showed us a model of divine restoration with the Father:

1. **The love of the Father** means the restoration of the relationship.
2. **Sonship** means to restore the status of the sons of God.
3. **The best robe** indicates the restoration of righteousness.
4. **The ring** symbolizes the restoration of authority.
5. **The sandals** represent the restoration of calling and purpose.
6. **The provision** is the restoration of finances and inheritance.
7. **Rejoicing and delighting in God** brings the restoration of the Tabernacle of David.

The Father is restoring sons and daughters, bringing them back into right relationship with Him. The Father is endowing His people with righteousness, authority, and financial provision, and they are delighting their hearts in Him. Their joy and praise will overflow for Him!

In the parable, the father kills the fatted calf and says, "Set the table. Let's dance and rejoice—my heart is in this." I can envision the father walking around and saying, "Let's rejoice! My son, we have reason to celebrate! Rejoice, even if it annoys others. I've been silent for a long time, and they thought I was like them. But no, I am restoring everything!"

Here's what happened next:

> *Now his older son was in the field. And as he came and drew near to the house, he heard music and dancing. So he called one of the servants and asked what these things meant (Luke 15: 25-26).*

Just picture the older brother coming back from the field. In other words, he was coming back from a long mission trip where he preached his heart out and wore himself out working and serving—he was coming home as a hero of our time. His father's house always greeted him with stillness and a peaceful atmosphere. There was no place for unforeseen disruptions because everything followed a pre-approved schedule: a few uplifting songs, an inspiring message, and a humble prayer to conclude. It all lasts about two hours, then everyone goes home. This has been going on for centuries. But God didn't want that.

As soon as the prodigal son returns to sonship and takes his place in the father's house, the atmosphere is filled with joy, singing, and dancing. The older brother didn't just hear the singing but also the sound of dancing—it was so intense that it shook the entire house. He got closer and didn't go any further; instead, he sent his servant to scope out the situation and returned with a report:

> *And he said to him, 'Your brother has come, and because he has received him safe and sound, your father has killed the fatted calf.' But he was angry and would not go in. Therefore his father came out and pleaded with him (Luke 15:27-28).*

As the news broke, a particular reaction arose in the older brother, and what was inside his heart was revealed, "I worked hard tending to the flocks, yet my father killed 'my' calf for that other son of His. And I never received a goat to celebrate with my friends..." At that moment, jealousy, pride, and self-righteousness began to bubble up in him. I can picture his angry face, "I'm not going inside the house." But the father loved both his sons and left the celebration just to invite his older son to join in the abundance. Unfortunately, the older brother stubbornly resisted. He had his own opinion about how things should be, how fellowship with his father should feel, what worship should sound like, and how everyone should treat the prodigal son.

Three Reasons

What held the older brother back from joining the celebration? He didn't rejoice that his younger brother was restored, saved, and healed. Instead, the older brother was bothered by the **singing, dancing, and feasting.** These three things still trigger the entire religious system: Singing, dancing, and finances. Religion says, "All they want is to make music loud in church. All they want is to dance in church. All they want is to collect money at those gatherings." These three reasons hold many people back from entering the abundance the Father has under His lordship.

If you could only understand how much religion hates these things, "Why are they yelling? This isn't from God. The church isn't supposed to be this way. Christianity isn't supposed to be this way. Christianity should be serious, sorrowful, and miserable. And everyone should cry about their sins at every service and for as long as possible."

Jesus once said:

> *But woe to you, scribes and Pharisees, hypocrites! For you shut up the kingdom of heaven against men; for you neither*

> *go in yourselves, nor do you allow those who are entering to go in (Matthew 23:13).*

Then you hear those religious leaders comment, "Tell the youth to be quiet." "Don't pray in tongues in church." "You can't have drums in church; they're too loud. Someone might get offended and not like it." It's sad to see pastors adjusting everything to people's opinions. What's even going on? Is it worth trading God's breath for people's comfort? I have the impression that a snake is slithering around, trying to suffocate everything God wants to do. Time will pass, and those leaders will feel the difference. They may remember how, at first, they used to gather and witness the move of the Holy Spirit, but then, everything died down. The form of service remained the same, but they lost God's breath and the move of the Holy Spirit in their services. God took His breath from them and moved on, looking for those who will worship Him with pure hearts, ready to serve Him *as He wants*—He is ready to breathe His breath of life on them.

But we Never Used to Praise This Way

Don't get me wrong. I honor how worship and services were in previous generations. However, I have always been looking for what God is currently doing, where His attention is now, and where His gaze is today. Why? Because His breath will be there, too.

I remember when our ministry began to grow, more young people started joining services, and worship in the church began to change. In one service, the tangible presence of God filled the room. People started waving flags, dancing, jumping, clapping, and whistling. It's worth mentioning that not everybody was fond of this.

"What are you doing there? Whistlers. Dancers. Is this a church? You guys turned it into a club…"

"Who said that we can't worship God this way?"

You know what's interesting? All of this unfolded spontaneously. We didn't plan it. We weren't putting on a show. But then, suddenly, a wave of fear washed over me, and I thought, "What if I, as the head pastor, begin to stop this move of God just because someone might not like it?" I can almost guarantee that some time would pass, the atmosphere would change, and the breath of God would depart. Friend, it's not about what instruments you use or how you express your worship; all that is secondary. The main thing is to remember that it's His ministry, and we're here to worship Him.

I'll admit that there are moments during worship when I don't want someone screaming right next to me. For example, a few weeks ago, people started whistling loudly during worship, and you know what I thought? *Well, when the next leadership meeting comes, I'll gather them, and…* And at that moment, the Holy Spirit spoke to me and said:

"I'm restoring the Tabernacle of David. I'm restoring My lordship. When a person belongs to Me, their whole being does too. Who gave mankind the breath and ability to whistle?"

Some people associate whistling with the world or even with demons. But God says:

"I'm restoring everything. I AM the LORD."

Hear me out; everything will belong to Him in the last days. It is written:

> *…therefore glorify God in your body and in your spirit, which are God's (1 Corinthians 6:20).*

Everything should worship the Lord, not just our hands, but also our feet and the rest of our bodies. God will take everything back for Himself. God will restore everything.

I want to say the following with great respect to the older generation. With my own eyes, I've seen grandmothers praising God in such a way that youth would be intimidated. It was to the point that I stood next to them and felt I was religious and conservative. I meet such grandmothers all over the world. So, age isn't an excuse to praise God; it has to do with a person's mindset and revelation of God's lordship.

Let me clear this up right away—I'm not in any way telling you to start jumping and whistling in church or acting out some other things in services. No! Don't fake it! Don't work this up artificially. But when the Holy Spirit moves on people, and God breathes on this worship, who am I to stop what He's doing?

It's easy to stop this, but getting it back afterward is impossible. You can ban youth from gathering in houses, singing certain songs, and implementing new ideas, methods, or expressions. You can stop it, but it would be impossible to restore this fresh breath, hunger, and zeal for God later. This is why I, as a minister, never want to try stopping or controlling what the Holy Spirit is doing.

If we surrender our ministry to God's lordship, He will keep breathing. The methods of service and expressions of worship will change, and that's fine. God is restoring everything He wants to see in His Church. Keep your eyes on God. He's breathing.

Some may point out:

"But we've never worshiped this way before."

"Have you ever thought that maybe God wasn't happy with how things were 50 years ago? After all, the full lordship of God wasn't embraced back then. Perhaps the way they worshiped was influenced by their circumstances, preferences, and past experiences."

What truly matters is where God is breathing right now, not where He was 100 years ago and especially not what people think about us.

The Giver of Life

God prompted me to talk about this because, without the breath of God, we will become a dead church and an empty religion. It doesn't matter if it's a Catholic or Charismatic congregation, Pentecostal, Baptist, or something else. Unfortunately, today, some charismatic churches have no breath of God. God doesn't want concerts. God doesn't desire performances. God always wanted His Church to be filled with His glory and to be able to do His will. He wanted the Church to demonstrate the power and anointing of the Holy Spirit, not our own abilities.

We shouldn't be focusing on methods. We should all focus on what God is breathing on right now. Look at what the prophet Isaiah writes:

> *Thus says God the Lord, who created the heavens and stretched them out, who spread forth the earth and that which comes from it, who gives breath to the people on it, and spirit to those who walk on it: "I, the Lord, have called You in righteousness, and will hold Your hand; I will keep You and give You as a covenant to the people, as a light to the Gentiles, to open blind eyes, to bring out prisoners from the prison, those who sit in darkness from the prison house. I am the Lord, that is My name; and My glory I will not give to another, nor My praise to carved images.*

Behold, the former things have come to pass, and new things I declare; before they spring forth I tell you of them."

Sing to the Lord a new song, and His praise from the ends of the earth, you who go down to the sea, and all that is in it, you coastlands and you inhabitants of them! (Isaiah 42:5-10).

There is a praise already directed towards the Lord, and this is the praise that we must join our voices to. We just read: *"Sing to the Lord a new song."* **A new song does not mean a new style but a new revelation of who God is.** A new song symbolizes a new season, connected to every tribe and tongue. Further, we read:

Let the wilderness and its cities lift up their voice, the villages that Kedar inhabits. Let the inhabitants of Sela sing, let them shout from the top of the mountains. Let them give glory to the Lord, and declare His praise in the coastlands (Isaiah 42:11-12).

The Holy Spirit is restoring this kind of worship across the face of the earth, and all people will come to know the living God—cities, islands, wilderness, villages, coastlands, and mountaintops. Despite everything happening in the world, when darkness covers the earth, His people who know His name will arise. They will restore the Tabernacle of David. Their attention won't be on the visible world but on Who God is. Their words, music, voices, might, and all their focus will be on the Lord and what He is doing at that moment. This will invoke heaven's reaction, and something would come out of this praise:

The LORD shall go forth like a mighty man; He shall stir up His zeal like a man of war. He shall cry out, yes, shout aloud; He shall prevail against His enemies (Isaiah 42:13).

Let me ask you: "Where will the Lord come from?" He's not hanging out somewhere in the clouds. He is inside you with all His glory, power, and might. He dwells in you through His Spirit. Do you know how His glory will be released? It will be through your words and your praise. You may be anticipating the arrival of an anointed man or woman of God to lay hands on you and pray, but God is eagerly waiting for you to recognize that His power and glory are already in you. The glory of God is not released only on stages; it comes from the inside of you, too. The praise in your mouth will release the Lord, mighty in battle, and He will restore courage, zeal, passion, and fire inside your temple. This zeal isn't something you can conjure up. This zeal is a gift that only God Himself can give you. God will awaken jealousy, shout aloud, and raise a battle cry. I don't even want to apologize to people who don't like what I'm shouting. I'm sorry, but I'm not worshiping you. Having tasted the goodness of God, I refuse to whisper my praise. I am a voice crying out in the wilderness: *Prepare the way of the Lord!*

You may be in this season to praise and worship God, and when you do—He will fight for you. If you're going through the wilderness right now and asking, "God, I've tried everything. What do even I do at this point?" Despite your problems, sing about the goodness of God. Despite all your enemies, sing to your Lord. Sing in the midst of every sickness; don't sing about how God can heal you, sing that He is your Healer. Sing in the middle of every oppression, not about how He can deliver you but that He is your Deliverer. God says, "I Myself will come forth from your praise, like a Man of War!" Through this praise, you will receive answers for long-standing problems in your life. It doesn't matter how much the devil stole, killed, and destroyed. God will come forth from your praise and deliver, restore, and return to you all that was lost and more.

Further, it is written:

I have held My peace a long time, I have been still and restrained Myself. Now I will cry like a woman in labor, I will pant and gasp at once (Isaiah 42:14).

In other words, God says, "Don't identify Me with the last season or with how things were 50 or 100 years ago. I have been still and restrained Myself for a long time. Now, I will cry like a woman in labor, panting and gasping."

We are entering a new season where we will not gather around the glory of men and their talents but around Him. Every song, instrument, sound, method, form, expression, message, and movement will be to Him, around Him, and for Him. I pray that His glory will shake everything in your life and that your life will be filled with His presence. I pray that you will become a carrier of God's glory and power!

Today, God's hands are restoring the Tabernacle of David and authentic worship, joy, celebration, and delight in God. His house will be filled with His *Shekinah glory* and the cloud of glory until heaven is one with the earth. God will constantly breathe on us, and every nation will come and worship the Only, Great, All-Powerful *LORD* of heaven and earth, the Great I AM.

Worthy. You alone are worthy. You are our LORD and our God. You are above everything as the Sovereign One. All glory be to You! All the praise be to You! All the worship is Yours, forever and ever!

Chapter 10
Not of This World

My food is to do the will of Him who sent Me, and to finish His work.

John 4:34

Not long ago, I flew back from another trip to Africa, where we held a big crusade and served many people. God has called me to equip His Church and to carry His fire all over the world, and this is why I travel a lot with my team, organize crusades, and serve at conferences, schools, and seminars in different countries. And every time I see God revealing His glory and performing incredible miracles, healings, and deliverances. Most importantly, people get saved. Praise the Lord for everything He does!

When I came home, I rolled my suitcase into the house and stopped at the door. My first thought was, "I need to go on a retreat with God and spend time with Him." You may ask, "Why? You just got back from a long trip. Why would you leave again? The trip went well, and God moved powerfully; you saw His glory and victory in that city…" Why did I need to leave again? It's because seeking the Lord after conferences, services, and crusades is just as important as praying and seeking God before them. Once I realized this truth, guarding my inner condition after those victories became just as important as what I did before those events. Regrettably, some ministers tend to unwind, relax, become complacent, and even fall into sin because they neglect to seek God in their secret place after moments of great victory or breakthrough. We all need to rest and recover, but never let your guard down spiritually. If you are a minister, cultivate a habit of taking retreats with the Lord after powerful services and moments when the Spirit of God moved through you. You need to hear His voice and allow Him to speak to you, direct you, reset you, and renew your spirit. The Holy Spirit taught me this principle from the Word:

> *At evening, when the sun had set, they brought to Him all who were sick and those who were demon-possessed. And the whole city was gathered together at the door. Then He healed many who were sick with various diseases, and cast out many demons; and He did not allow the demons to speak, because they knew Him. Now in the morning, having risen a long while before daylight, He went out and departed to a solitary place; and there He prayed. And Simon and those who were with Him searched for Him. When they found Him, they said to Him, 'Everyone is looking for You.' But He said to them, 'Let us go into the next towns, that I may preach there also, because for this purpose I have come forth'* (Mark 1:32-38).

Think about all the commotion that started when the whole city gathered! There were people of different ages, professions, and social statuses. Everyone assembled there, not just those who believed in Jesus. Everyone! Some people didn't understand what was happening; they just followed the crowd. People also brought their sick, lame, blind, and demon-possessed. Everyone in the city was drawn to His light. And everywhere Jesus went, God's light, divine transformation, and the gospel of the Kingdom followed Him. That evening, He ministered a lot. Just imagine what people experienced in that place. What an atmosphere: the presence of God, glory, joy, and miracles, this was a massive revival!

But the following morning, Jesus wasn't in the house. He left early to go to a secluded place to spend time with His Father. The disciples found Him and joyfully exclaimed, "People are waiting for You! They have testimonies and want to experience God's power again. Yesterday was amazing! So... are you done praying? Come with us! Everyone's inviting us. The whole city will gather again—it's a revival! Hallelujah!"

Jesus ignored their words and responded, "We're going further to other cities and villages because God has other plans. I'm pursuing the Father's will." This is everything! The Bible says that *the Son can do nothing of Himself, but what He sees the Father do* (see John 5:19). This is why He abided in prayer after that night of powerful ministry. His attention was on the Father, His heart, His voice, and His guidance. And here come Jesus' disciples, eager to tell Him what the people want.

Place yourself in Jesus' position. What if, after an excellent service, you hear:

"Everyone's talking about that powerful revival service you led. There are so many testimonies of healing and miracles. The whole city is eagerly waiting for you again, and people are asking you to come back and preach again!"

"Who, me? The whole city?"

Reflecting on these words, you begin to feel excited, encouraged, and inspired, so you reply:

"Wow! Are the pastors and leaders asking for me, too?"

"Absolutely!"

"Really?! What else are they saying?"

Do you know what that's called? It's called feeding your ego and soul. Friend, this kind of attention can be dangerous. I'm not saying you must refuse it, but you should "close" your heart to the praise. Hear it, but don't listen to it. This isn't the source you should feed or nourish your inner self with; otherwise, you'll start to let yourself be led by people's words and praises. Ministers cannot allow people's praises to become a source of motivation. Otherwise, there is the risk of focusing on what people say and aligning themselves with what people want.

Jesus must become our prime example in everything. After that mighty move of God, He retreated with the Father and prayed, saying:

My food is to do the will of Him who sent Me, and to finish His work (John 4:34).

In other words, He was saying, "The Father is My source. My nourishment comes from doing His will, not from hearing people's kind words or high praises. I hear the Father and do His will. All My attention is on Him."

Suppose we, as ministers, allow ourselves to indulge in spiritual complacency even in the slightest. In that case, we won't notice how we divert our focus from God to people and lean towards pleasing them. I want to highlight again: Jesus' attention was directed solely toward the will of His Father and what the Father was doing. We should be the same way.

When your attention is on the Father and His will, you will want to serve people. But when your attention is on people, you will want to please people.

There is a fine line here, and to understand what's going on in your heart, you need to pull yourself out of the crowd, retreat with God, and realign your attention, motives, and priorities with His. In addition to our daily relationships with God, we must learn to stop everything and retreat with the Lord. Make it a habit. Retreat with God to spend time fasting and praying, standing on guard, holding your spiritual position, surrendering to the Lord, and saying, "Lead me further.", especially after big conferences and projects. That's what Jesus did. That will help you to maintain complete dependence on the Lord. Remember: because He does His work through you, all the glory is His too.

Despite all the victories and power of God, I see in my life, I always come to His presence in a position of humility and complete surrender.

I'll never forget what God told me once:

"Never enter into My presence as an apostle, prophet, or a pastor."

I thought about it and asked Him:

"Holy Spirit, what do you mean?"

"Enter into My presence as a son coming to the Father."

Always come to God's presence without any sense of entitlement or self-righteousness. We shouldn't use our titles to draw near to Him, and certainly shouldn't have the older son's attitude in the parable in Luke 15, who returned home feeling justified and self-righteous. Let's enter His presence with an open and humble heart. Even when you serve God a lot, if you stop growing in the knowledge of Him, then sooner or later, you may eventually adopt the mindset of the older son. He based his righteousness solely on his works, which is why he spent all his time in serving the Father instead of cultivating a genuine relationship with him. This is not what our Heavenly Father expects from us!

Remember, ministry doesn't give you the right to be closer to God than others. Your good works don't provide you with access to a more intimate relationship with God. Your position in the church doesn't bring you closer to God, either. Only His grace does! We come closer to Him by grace. **Only by His grace!** Here lies the foundation of our intimacy with Him (see Ephesians, chapter 2). You can't earn or serve your way into intimacy with God.

In a personal relationship with God, you come to Him as a son or a daughter, not a ministry leader. But when He sends you to do His work and fulfill His will on earth, you step out and operate in your status, as an apostle, pastor, prophet, evangelist, teacher, etc.

Three Elements

Throughout this book, we have discussed praying in the secret place, creating a close relationship with God, and living under His lordship. However, besides prayer, I have two additional practices I also do in secret—they take me to a completely different level in God. I don't want to end this book without sharing these things with you.

These two practices are fasting and sacrificial giving. These three elements (prayer, fasting, and giving) increase the fruit in my life thirty, sixty, and one hundredfold. They are like a threefold cord that is not easily broken.

Fasting

Why is fasting important in your relationship with God? Let me clarify: fasting is not about food—*food does not bring us near to God; we are no worse if we do not eat and no better if we do* (1 Corinthians 8:8 NIV). Fasting is about dealing with our flesh, or more precisely, with the desires of the flesh. Perhaps you've noticed that after a big meal, your body feels heavy, and your spiritual senses are usually dulled. If you constantly overeat and don't fast, your physical senses overpower your spiritual senses. Food sort of "weighs down" and blurs your spiritual perception. However, fasting silences the voice of your flesh and gives more room to your spirit.

You fast to free yourself **from** something and give yourself **to** something else. You free yourself from physical food to hear God's voice and be sensitive to the Holy Spirit. You humble yourself to be closer to God so you can listen to His voice, His leading, and His promptings. In the process, the will of God becomes your food.

Unfortunately, many believers associate fasting solely with resolving problems and getting through hard times. More than once, I've heard such comments, "You're fasting? Oh no, what's wrong? Do you have problems?" People usually fast to overcome sin or to intensify their pleading before God to resolve their hardship. And yes, fervent prayer paired with fasting definitely helps. Throughout the Bible, people practiced this kind of fasting and received powerful answers. But I've always been curious not just to learn about people's experiences but to learn the God's ways and how He sees fasting. Why did Jesus fast? What did Jesus Himself say about this? After all, Jesus is the true Light that gives light to every man coming into the world. He brought us a new covenant with God. He gave us access to the Kingdom of God and led us further into knowing the Father. What did Jesus say about fasting? Why is fasting necessary in God's Kingdom? Why does fasting matter?

In the Gospel of Matthew, chapters 5, 6, and 7, Jesus lays out the principles of the Kingdom of God. These three chapters are one sermon, the Sermon on the Mount, which was only later broken up into three chapters. So, we must look at those chapters as one message in which Jesus teaches us the principles of the Kingdom of God and leads us into the complete lordship of God. In these chapters, Jesus talks about prayer, fasting, and sacrificial giving. Okay, we already talked about prayer in secret, let's delve into fasting:

> *But you, when you fast, anoint your head and wash your face, so that you do not appear to men to be fasting, but to your Father who is in the secret place; and your Father who sees in secret will reward you openly (Matthew 6:17-18).*

First, note that Jesus said *when* you fast, not *if* you fast. In other words, in the concept of the Kingdom of God, prayer, fasting, and giving are part of our lifestyle; they're not optional. Jesus didn't say "if." He taught **when** you fast, **when** you pray, and **when** you give. In heaven, we will not fast, pray, or give sacrificially. Thus, these elements are necessary for our time here on earth and should become our way of life here.

Second, Jesus taught that the focus of fasting was to draw closer to Him. In Luke 5:33-35 it says:

> *Then they said to Him, "Why do the disciples of John fast often and make prayers, and likewise those of the Pharisees, but Yours eat and drink?"*
>
> *And He said to them, "Can you make the friends of the bridegroom fast while the bridegroom is with them? But the days will come when the bridegroom will be taken away from them; then they will fast in those days."*

This passage holds an important truth: the disciples will fast when the bridegroom is taken away from them, meaning when Jesus physically leaves the earth. In other words, Jesus was saying, "I'm here right now; that's why they don't need to fast. But when the time comes for Me to leave this world, then they will need to fast to stay close to Me."

Fasting is more than just a problem-solving tool. I fast to draw closer to the Lord, get to know Him, and present myself to Him so He can deal with my heart and inner condition. When I fast, my only goal is to hear and see the Lord and for His desires to become mine. I believe God has enormous plans, and I don't want to miss anything because of my flesh or inability to hear Him.

Third, you don't need to wait for a particular word from God to start fasting at least once a week or three days a month. God revealed this principle in Scripture. When God created this world, He gave a day of rest to all creation—man, animal, and earth. I believe that applies to our bodies as well. God designed our bodies to have time to rest from food, whether one day a week or one day a month. Our physical bodies need breaks, too. Fasting can help our spiritual man maintain a healthy walk with the Lord, deepen our spiritual awareness, and improve our spiritual health, enabling us to hear God more clearly. When we abstain from food, we may start to notice that our spiritual senses are heightened, our dreams become vivid, and we become more sensitive to the voice of God, noticing Him in everything. That is why taking short fasts (like 1-2 days) should become routine for us. Longer fasts are different. I firmly believe that you should only take them when the Holy Spirit leads you there. And every person must be led by the Lord in their fasting journey.

If you have any health issues, seek professional advice and consult your doctor before starting any fast. Use wisdom in your decisions. I'm not a medical professional, and this book is not a medical guide.

Again, fasting means replacing physical food with spiritual food, connecting with God, and hearing His voice so He can guide you toward His will. And when we fast with this understanding and desire Him more than we desire physical food, then the Word of God and His will has become our nourishment. Jesus says in John 4:34: *"My food is to do the will of Him who sent Me, and to finish His work."* In other words, He's saying: "Doing the Father's will nourishes Me. He is My source of life." By the way, He said this after ministering to the Samaritan woman at the well (see John 4). And before that, Jesus was physically tired and hungry! What happened?

After a long journey, Jesus made a stop at the well because He was hungry and weary from the road. Meanwhile, all His disciples went into the city to buy food. When the Samaritan woman came to the well to draw water, Jesus began to minister the Word and do the will of God, and suddenly His hunger was satisfied. I'll say more: The Samaritan woman's thirst was quenched, too. Prior to this, Jesus was physically hungry, and the Samaritan woman was physically thirsty. He needed food. She needed water. But as soon as Jesus began to do the will of God, the Samaritan woman's thirst was quenched, and Jesus' hunger was satisfied.

She left her jar and went away into the town with no water. When the disciples came back with the food, offering some to Jesus, He replied, "I'm all set, I'm not hungry anymore." The disciples were puzzled and said to one another, "What does He mean? Who brought Him food?" Like the disciples, many of us don't fully understand the concept of spiritual food. We sometimes fail to realize how much the spiritual food that comes from doing the will of God is able to satisfy our need for physical nourishment. When we make God's will our priority, it becomes our sustenance.

We truly start living when we begin fulfilling the will of God.

The lifestyle of prayer, fasting, and giving allows God to lead you deeper and further into intimacy with Him and to fulfill His will.

Giving

In the same 6th chapter of Matthew where Jesus taught about prayer and fasting, He continues with the following:

> *Do not lay up for yourselves treasures on earth, where moth and rust destroy and where thieves break in and steal; but lay up for yourselves treasures in heaven, where neither moth nor rust destroys and where thieves do not break in and steal. For where your treasure is, there your heart will be also (Matthew 6: 19-21).*

Your treasure and your heart are linked to one another. Where your treasure is, your attention will also be; your worship and your heart will be there, too. You don't have to try and prove to me how much you love God or declare your willingness to serve Him with all your heart. Show me your checkbook and I will show you where your heart is. Your heart and your treasure share an unbreakable bond.

Jesus continues:

> *No one can serve two masters; for either he will hate the one and love the other, or else he will be loyal to the one and despise the other. You cannot serve God and mammon (Matthew 6:24).*

The word "mammon" is borrowed from the Greek and means "wealth" and "riches." Jesus said, "You will not be able to serve both God and wealth."

I've noticed that mammon always tries to stand in the way of God's full lordship in a person's life. Unfortunately, many believers today are enslaved by mammon to one degree or another. I came to realize that neither prayer nor fasting can free you from mammon; only sacrificial giving can. I'm not talking about tithing, offering, or making a donation. I'm talking about a sacrifice that will cost you everything and free your heart for the lordship of God.

The Holy Spirit began to teach me these things through simple steps of obedience. Every time God led me to make a sacrifice, He brought me to a new level of knowledge, dominion, and intimacy with Him. It's a remarkable process in which reliance on the physical world lessens, and His lordship over my life amplifies. True sonship is impossible without sacrifice.

I remember one day when God told me to give away all the money I had saved for a new car. When He told me to sow my savings, He freed me from dependence on the visible world and led me into dependence on the invisible God. The point is not the amount but the obedience to God.

As usual, I came to the office one day and began to pray. I walked around the office, asking God to guide me in my personal life and in my ministry. After the prayer, I checked my emails and messages. I saw a video of a pastor I knew on a social media platform, asking for financial support for his project. Although it was a commendable project that aimed to spread the Kingdom of God, I wasn't planning to donate at all.

I didn't think about it because I had my own ministry and my own projects. And suddenly, I heard God's voice within me, "Take out all the money you've been saving for a car and give it all to him." I froze... Let me explain so you understand my situation better. I owned an old car that I drove my little daughter to school in daily. She had just started school. And one day, when I was driving her, she said, "Daddy, don't go all the way to school. Stop a little before." I usually dropped her off right at the entrance. She explained, "Dad, we have such an old car; it's embarrassing." My six-year-old girl told me, "Dad, I'm embarrassed that you take me to school in this old car." I laughed, but felt uncomfortable. After she got out of the car, I said to the Lord, "God, we need to do something about this. I need a new car."

So, my wife and I started saving money for a car (I can't remember exactly how much we saved). We couldn't afford to buy a new car, so I was going to trade this one in for something better. And then, I heard God say to me, "Take everything in your savings and give it to this pastor."

When God tells you to sacrifice, you'll start to feel deep inside that you'll regret if you don't give. And secondly, you no longer feel like it's your money—you still have that money, but it doesn't feel like it's yours anymore.

When God tells me to do something, I try to respond immediately. Obedience to the voice of God is always important to me. Usually, if I feel that God is asking me to give something, I won't even think twice. But this time was different because I saved the money together with my wife. I was also thinking of my daughter. I remembered her words. That's why I started praying about it more, "Lord, give me a confirmation. I'm going to call Natasha, and if she says, "Yes, Andrey, do it," then that's my sign to immediately write the check and give it to this minister."

So, I called my wife, she was at work at that time, she picked up the phone and I said:

"Natasha, I was just praying and felt God wanted us to do something."

She answered:

"Oh, my God... What is it this time?"

This was her normal reaction, since we had already gone through different moments in our life and ministry.

"Something we have never done before."

"Andrey, don't scare me!"

"I feel God wants us to give all the money we saved in the account to one minister."

Then I told her about that project.

"Are you sure this was God speaking?"

"Well, as far as I understand, it was the Lord. I heard Him…"

"Then write the check and give it to the pastor."

I didn't think about anything else. I immediately wrote the check, got into my car—the same car I used to drive my daughter to school every day, and went to see that minister. I walked into his office, put a check on his desk, and said, "God told me to give you this money for your project."

It's interesting that on the way back, I felt a wave of joy wash over me; it was unlike anything I had ever experienced. It seems completely backwards to the people of this world, "What are you happy about? You have no more money left in your account, yet you're rejoicing…"

Nevertheless, inside, I knew God was pleased. I heard His voice saying, "You have no idea what a privilege it is to sacrifice and be a part of My work on this earth. Others would like to, but they don't have the opportunity. But I gave you this opportunity."

At that moment, I began to see the difference between the types of lordships that Jesus taught: the lordship of the visible world and the invisible world. Through sacrifice, God frees us from the grip of the visible world's power and grants us access to the power and authority of the invisible world. If I had not practiced this myself, I would not have the audacity to write about it.

By the way, not much time passed before God orchestrated a series of events in my life where He sent people who generously blessed me with financial gifts without knowledge of my needs; suddenly, this unexpected provision granted me the opportunity to purchase a much better car than I could have bought myself with the money we saved.

So, what does sacrifice do?

Firstly, sacrifice makes room in your heart for God's lordship and turns your heart towards the eternal values of God's Kingdom. We do not buy God with our sacrifice—on the contrary, we open ourselves up to a higher dependency on His lordship in our lives.

Secondly, every time God told me to sacrifice, He showed me the "fertile soil" to sow into, and it always had to do with advancing the Kingdom of God. You sow where you want to go. You sow where you want to reap. You do not throw your precious seed into any ground or place, but you put it in the good, fruitful soil that God shows you.

Thirdly, whenever God told me to sacrifice, I knew He was leading me into a new season. I saw this spiritual principle in the Scripture. When Solomon made a sacrifice pleasing to God, the Lord came to him in a dream and transferred him to a new season (see 1 Kings 3:4-14). Cornelius, a pagan centurion, gave alms generously and had a prayer life dedicated to God. His faith and benevolence caught the Lord's attention (see Acts 10). Consequently, God dispatched an angel and the apostle Peter to guide Cornelius into a new season of his life.

Remember, it's not about the amount you give; it's all about obeying His voice. Obedience to God is better than sacrifice. Through your obedience, God begins to lead you to do His will step by step. Sacrifice plays a crucial role in this process.

We all have our own measures of sacrifice, and the Holy Spirit aims to lead us to them and set our hearts free for Him. In this process, God recognizes our individuality. Therefore, don't copy other people's sacrifices. The point is not the amount; what matters is your obedience. The size of our offerings doesn't impress God. But faith that simply obeys Him and surrenders to His lordship does impress Him. Therefore, do not give everything to God, but give everything He tells you to give.

There has never been a time in my life when God told me to sacrifice, and I obeyed, but I didn't see His glory, faithfulness, and lordship manifest. He is the Lord and Master who gives me life, and everything I have serves His purposes and Kingdom.

The Father of Faith

God wants to lead you further into your destiny to fulfill His will. He will guide you with His voice and expect your obedience. Reread the story of Abraham. It is written:

> "And Abram believed the LORD, and the LORD counted him as righteous because of his faith" (Genesis 15:6 NLT).

His faith was expressed in obedience, not just words. Abraham obeyed the Lord, left Ur of the Chaldeans behind, and ventured to an unknown land. It was a one—way ticket from his homeland and father's house to the destiny God had for him. Abraham surrendered himself to the Lord completely.

Abraham's faith was expressed not only in words but in wholehearted obedience to the Lord. Obedience requires sacrifice, and each sacrifice symbolizes the death of our desires and ambitions. In other words, obedience means the denial of our flesh, which is the sacrifice itself. Just as a seed must die to sprout and then flourish, we, too, must die to ourselves and rise again for the glory of God to manifest through us. This act of obedience is a pleasing sacrifice to Him.

On the journey of consecration, God tested Abraham's faith, asking Him for the ultimate sacrifice: his son Isaac. The question arises, "Why Isaac?" Because God's vision extended far beyond Abraham's life. He saw the fulfillment of His perfect and pleasing will through Abraham, birthing His people on earth. God saw the potential to accomplish His will through Abraham's willingness to sacrifice his son.

God did not want to take Isaac away. He wanted Isaac to become a "seed," a blessing for all nations. For this to happen, Abraham had to free his heart from Isaac and surrender to the complete lordship of God. So, God led Abraham:

"Abraham, I promised you a son at the beginning of your journey."

"Yes, God."

"My thoughts go beyond personal blessings. My will is to bless you and bring a blessing to the earth through you that will transcend generations. Abraham, it's not just about you. This seed will be a blessing to all nations. But there is a spiritual principle: unless the seed dies, it cannot produce life. To accomplish My will, I require something of you."

"God, do it. Your will be done," Abraham unwaveringly trusted and obeyed God.

"Abraham, the people of this world will fail to understand it. Your kin and neighbors will not comprehend it. Only a man of faith will understand. Your mindset came to that condition when you, contrary to hope, in hope believed. Only you and I will fathom this truth. Just as I brought you out of the Ur of the Chaldeans and blessed you with Isaac, in the same way, I am now leading you further into My divine plan. Take your beloved son and journey to the mountain where you shall offer him as a sacrifice to Me.

> *Then He said, "Take now your son, your only son Isaac, whom you love, and go to the land of Moriah, and offer him there as a burnt offering on one of the mountains of which I shall tell you" (Genesis 22:2).*

An ordinary person's first reaction would be, "God, how can You ask for such a thing? After all, this is the promised son, the heir, and Abraham's treasure!"

Abraham loved Isaac wholeheartedly. God did not want Isaac to be killed physically. Remember that it is written, "Where your treasure is, there your heart will be also." God needed to take Abraham's heart and place it in another treasure. He wanted to connect Abraham's heart to what eye cannot see and ear cannot hear.

To accomplish this, God required total obedience. Abraham needed to offer a sacrifice of such a magnitude that it would bring forth the people of God, His generation, and the faith of God that calls into being the things that don't exist yet, gives life to the dead, and can fulfill the will of the Lord. Through this sacrifice and test of faith, these elements were imprinted upon the seed of Isaac.

> *The next morning Abraham got up early. He saddled his donkey and took two of his servants with him, along with his son, Isaac. Then he chopped wood for a fire for a burnt offering and set out for the place God had told him about.*

On the third day of their journey, Abraham looked up and saw the place in the distance (Genesis 22:3-4 NLT).

Reading this passage, I want to say to him:

"Abraham, your journey to the mountain will change you forever. Your act of faith and obedience will place the hand of the Lord upon your son, his descendants, and the next generations so that God's will can be fulfilled."

"Stay here with the donkey," Abraham told the servants. "The boy and I will travel a little farther. We will worship there, and then we will come right back."

So Abraham placed the wood for the burnt offering on Isaac's shoulders, while he himself carried the fire and the knife. As the two of them walked on together (Genesis 22:5-6 NLT).

The fact is that the servants did not go further! Yes! The servants stayed at the bottom of the mountain with the donkey, and Abraham went to worship God. I want to emphasize again that only Abraham and his sacrifice climbed further up the mountain!

Let me explain this picture prophetically: there is a place where God wants to raise you as a son or a daughter so that he can start a new generation through you. However, to reach that place, you must leave everything behind. Only you and your sacrifice can go further up the mountain—only you and your sacrifice!

So Abraham placed the wood for the burnt offering on Isaac's shoulders, while he himself carried the fire and the knife. As the two of them walked on together, Isaac turned to Abraham and said, "Father?"

"Yes, my son?" Abraham replied.

> *"We have the fire and the wood," the boy said, "but where is the sheep for the burnt offering?"*
>
> *"God will provide a sheep for the burnt offering, my son," Abraham answered. And they both walked on together (Genesis 22:6-8 NLT).*

Abraham replied, "My dear son, I don't fully understand, but I believe. I don't see the lamb yet, but God does, and He will provide the sacrifice."

The faith of God doesn't see what God takes away but what God takes to multiply. And much further through the ages, this spotless Lamb, through His obedience to God, would bring a perfect sacrifice to unite us forever with our Heavenly Father, and make us sons and daughters of God, the heirs of all His promises. Such is the power of obedience and sacrifice: it leaves an undeniable mark on our hearts and lives.

> *When they arrived at the place where God had told him to go, Abraham built an altar and arranged the wood on it. Then he tied his son, Isaac, and laid him on the altar on top of the wood. And Abraham picked up the knife to kill his son as a sacrifice. At that moment the angel of the LORD called to him from heaven, "Abraham! Abraham!"*
>
> *"Yes," Abraham replied. "Here I am!"*
>
> *"Don't lay a hand on the boy!" the angel said. "Do not hurt him in any way, for now I know that you truly fear God. You have not withheld from me even your son, your only son."*
>
> *Then Abraham looked up and saw a ram caught by its horns in a thicket. So he took the ram and sacrificed it as a burnt offering in place of his son (Genesis 22:9-13 NLT).*

God never wanted Abraham to kill Isaac physically! Abraham did not "kill" his son on the mountain; he "killed" him in his heart on the way up the mountain. And through this, God connected Abraham's heart to eternal heavenly values. The same happened with Jesus. Do you think Jesus died on the cross? Only His body died on the cross. Jesus died to Himself entirely in the Garden of Gethsemane so the will of God would be done; thus, He "died" on the way to Calvary.

When Abraham raised the knife, he saw the bound body of his son, and God through the ages saw the body of His Son, bound by sin, curse, and sickness. His Son took all the sin of the world upon Himself and gave Himself as a guilt offering and atonement for sin. The old nature died in Him, and when He rose, a new man emerged, created according to God. God saw that the Spirit of the Lord would quicken the Body, which would do His will here on earth as it is in heaven. Through Jesus' perfect sacrifice, **God foresaw the generation of the Lamb, one that is called and chosen by God, and not of this world.**

Isaiah prophesies about this matter, exclaiming, "Who will declare His generation?" It pleased the Lord to strike Him. God saw His generation as eternal and impervious to any interference of hell, demons, death, or anything else. His will will be accomplished here on earth as in heaven (see Isaiah 53).

When God saw that Abraham was obedient till the end and did not spare his only son, He said, "I promised you before, but now I swear to you!"

> *This is what the LORD says: Because you have obeyed me and have not withheld even your son, your only son, I swear by my own name that I will certainly bless you. I will multiply your descendants beyond number, like the stars in the sky and the sand on the seashore. Your descendants will conquer the cities of their enemies. And through your*

descendants all the nations of the earth will be blessed—all because you have obeyed me" (Genesis 22:16-18 NLT).

Note that God did not swear to him at first, but after the sacrifice, He swore by His own name, "Abraham, you did not spare your only son, but freed your heart so that I would sit on the throne of your heart. You gave Me a place! I swear this seed will not just come forth, but it will take dominion, power, and will rule. I will bless your seed so much that it will conquer its enemies, and all the peoples of the earth will be blessed through your seed."

And so, Abraham's journey led him to become the father of faith, and not just faith, but God's faith.

God is calling you to draw closer to Him, but only you and your sacrifice can go further up the mountain. You can't even fathom God's plans and dreams for your life! He wants to lift you and change your whole destiny. However, you cannot get there without complete dedication, full obedience, and total sacrifice—these three factors play a crucial role. The mindset of a servant or a slave won't ascend the mountain. You cannot go up there with your pastor, parents, best friend, or someone else's opinions. You must leave everything behind. It's your choice, willingness to be obedient, and your own personal sacrifice.

Throughout this book, the Lord dealt with your mindset and heart. Everything you read is not just information. God wants to manifest it all in your life—His lordship, glory, and greatness. God wants to transition you from one season to the next. There is only one path, and it requires your sacrifice. God says, "I will show you the place and the sacrifice. This sacrifice will connect your heart with Mine."

Do you want to see God's glory on this earth in your life? Surrender yourself to God in complete dedication, complete sacrifice, and complete obedience.

In this book, we talked a lot about having a close relationship with God, but this relationship must lead you to something—to live under the full lordship of God and to fulfill His will. The more you abide in Him, the more you will be transformed into His image, likeness, and nature; there will be less of you and more of God in you. Then you will be able to say: *"It is no longer I who live, but Christ lives in me"* (Galatians 2:20).

In today's Christianity, it has become customary for us to constantly wait for something—the glory of God to manifest, revival to unfold, or a great awakening to come... Have you ever asked yourself how it will all arrive? It will come through our complete surrender to God under His lordship! I'm convinced that both the coming revival and manifestation of His glory are directly related to our full dedication to the Lord. The greater the dedication, the greater the revival. The greater His lordship in our lives, the more His will is done through us. From His presence, God will begin to send you to do His will—you will not be a spectator; you will be an active participant!

I see in my spirit that God's generation is rising, sons and daughters who will devote themselves entirely to the Lord and do His works. They will be steadfast, trusting in the Lord, even when darkness overshadows the economy, politics, education, or other aspects of life. They will dismantle the devil's schemes and bring God's divine order and light to every corner of our society. They will bring heaven to earth, and His will shall reign supreme here as it is in heaven. God not only promises; He fulfills it too!

I see in my spirit that God is restoring the revelation of sonship and His Kingdom worldwide, which is correlated with the imminent last days Awakening and the last Great Harvest. Sonship is the core of our identity, and the Kingdom of God is our reality. If you are a son or daughter, you belong to the Kingdom. When you realize this truth, it becomes your responsibility to uphold your identity and spread the

Kingdom of God. Jesus, being aware of His responsibility, destroyed all the works of the enemy.

In the same way, God's sons and daughters will come out of His presence and destroy the works of the devil. They will see with the Father's eyes: crowds of people around them who are hungry, exhausted, weary, and unsaved. They all are His children, even if they live under a different lordship.

I see in my spirit that in the spiritual world, God is consecrating people for Himself right now; He is placing His hand on them and declaring, "They are Mine, My sons and daughters, My generation!"

Who has believed our report? Who will I trust with this? And to whom has the arm of the LORD been revealed? Who will declare My generation? To whom can I reveal My power to rebuild the old ruins, raise the former desolations, and repair the ruined cities, the desolations of many generations? I have held My silence for a long time; I have been still and restrained Myself. But I will no longer be silent. I will cry out like a woman in labor because I am giving birth to My people, My seed, My faith, and a generation after My heart! I will shout because I am birthing God's faith in the earth. These people will not be of this world— They are My sons and daughters, My generation!

Today, allow God to show you the sacrifice that will take you further in Him. He indicated the sacrifice to Abraham. He wants to show you the sacrifice that will take you into the next season of your life. Only He knows the measure that He wants to free your heart, and it is not the same for everyone. Today, I'm doing it with you. This is such a holy moment. Pause and let Him speak to your heart now. I'm not asking you to sow into my ministry; let God show you the soil where you should sow. We are making room for our future, and it is in God—our treasure will be in Him, and our sacrifice will link our hearts with His. I live by this principle from season to season, bringing a sacrificial offering to the

Lord so that He will be the Lord of my heart and so I can be a blessing to all nations, all people, and all languages—because this is the will of my Heavenly Father.

I want to finish this book on my knees:

Father, take me. I'm all yours. May Your fire fall on this sacrifice. From this moment on, my food is to do Your will and complete Your work on this earth. May a mighty generation, Your generation, be birthed through my life, a generation that will do Your will. God, I want to see millions of souls saved. I want to see Your glory on earth and be a part of Your Harvest and Your movement. I surrender myself to be Your hands, Your feet, and Your voice. I'm all yours. In Jesus name!

Father, I pray now that You consecrate the one reading this book. Precious Holy Spirit, lift this person to heights beyond their reach. Encounter them, put Your hand on their lives, and mark them for Yourself. I pray that You will uproot everything in them that was not planted by You, restoring them to sonship. May their dedication to You cause Your glory to descend this generation. May they start living in such a way that You would say of them, *"This is My son, this is My daughter, this is My generation."*

Father, seal, confirm, and fulfill this word in their lives. In the mighty name of Jesus Christ. Amen.

This isn't goodbye, this is see you later!

With love,

Andrey

Stay Connected

www.facebook.com/AndreyShapovalPage

www.instagram.com/itsandreyshapoval

www.youtube.com/ffministry

If you have a testimony from reading this book, please email andrey@ffministry.com

If you would like to know more about Andrey Shapoval ministry or become a part of this vision, visit our website www.shapovalministries.com

We invite you to attend our annual Kingdom Domain school. Registration and details are on the website www.kingdomdomain.com

If your organization or church would like to invite Andrey Shapoval to speak at an event, contact our ministry office. We would gladly consider your invitation!

admin@ffministry.com
+1(916) 472-0847
+1(916) 338-3390

Other Books

PREDESTINED

Born for Greatness

BIG GOD

When God becomes bigger than your reality

Available everywhere books are sold in paperback, electronic, audio version. For more information on international distribution and/or translation to other languages visit www.ffministry.com/books or email lubakasy@ffministry.com